LONDON
A Very
Peculiar History™

With added jellied eels

'London is a roost for every bird.'
Benjamin Disraeli
(British Prime Minister,
1868 and 1874–1880)

To the joys of London: Club Tone, one pound to
Balham, and missing the last night bus...

JP

Editor: Stephen Haynes
Additional artwork: Penko Gelev, Nick Hewetson,
Pam Hewetson, John James, Mark Peppé, Gerald Wood

Published in Great Britain in MMX by
Book House, an imprint of
The Salariya Book Company Ltd
25 Marlborough Place, Brighton BN1 1UB
www.salariya.com
www.book-house.co.uk

HB ISBN-13: 978-1-907184-26-0

© The Salariya Book Company Ltd MMX

3 5 7 9 8 6 4 2
A CIP catalogue record for this book is available
from the British Library.
Printed and bound in Dubai.
Printed on paper from sustainable sources.
Reprinted MMXI

Visit our website at **www.book-house.co.uk**
or go to **www.salariya.com**
for **free** electronic versions of:
You Wouldn't Want to be an Egyptian Mummy!
You Wouldn't Want to be a Roman Gladiator!
Avoid Joining Shackleton's Polar Expedition!
Avoid Sailing on a 19th-Century Whaling Ship!

WARNING: The Salariya Book Company accepts
no responsibility for the historical recipes in this
book. They are included only for their historical
interest and may not be suitable for modern use.

LONDON
A Very Peculiar History™

With added jellied eels

Written by
Jim Pipe

Illustrated by
David Antram

Created and designed by
David Salariya

and

Mark Bergin

'When a man is tired
of London, he is tired of life;
for there is in London all that
life can afford.'
Dr Samuel Johnson (1709–1784)

'That great foul city of London
– rattling, growling, smoking,
stinking – ghastly heap of
fermenting brickwork, pouring
out poison at every pore...'
John Ruskin (1819–1900)

'The streets of London,
to be beheld at the very height
of their glory, should be seen
on a dark dull murky
winter's night.'
Charles Dickens, *Sketches by Boz*
(1836)

'London has the effect of
making one feel historic.'
V. S. Pritchett (1900–1997)

Contents

Putting London on the map

1. **50,000 BC:** River Thames pushed into its present course by ice sheet.
2. **AD 70:** Roman amphitheatre built near the site of the present Guildhall.
3. **604:** First St Paul's Cathedral built (current building finished 1710).
4. **800:** Anglo-Saxon town of Ludenwic stood where Covent Garden is now.
5. **1065:** Westminster Abbey built by pious king Edward the Confessor.
6. **1078:** William the Conqueror starts work on Tower of London.
7. **1176:** London Bridge rebuilt in stone.
8. **1381:** Wat Tyler, leader of Peasants' Revolt. is killed in Smithfield market.
9. **1422:** Lincoln's Inn founded, making Holborn the home of legal London.
10. **1599:** Theatre-goers flock to the Globe Theatre (reconstructed 1997).
11. **1649:** King Charles I loses his head outside Whitehall Palace.
12. **1666:** The Monument commemorates the Great Fire of this year.
13. **1734:** Bank of England moves to its current site in Threadneedle St.
14. **1780:** Gordon Riots – mob breaks into Newgate prison, where Old Bailey criminal courts are today.
15. **1819:** Piccadilly Circus becomes hub of West End's shopping district.
16. **1837:** Queen Victoria first makes Buckingham Palace a royal home.
17. **1859:** Clock tower containing Big Ben completes new Houses of Parliament.
18. **1905:** Harrods department store opens its doors in Knightsbridge.
19. **1966:** Swinging London: 500,000 flock to Rolling Stones concert in Hyde Park.
20. **1991:** Canary Wharf Tower becomes a symbol for rebuilt Docklands.
21. **1999:** London Eye marks the new millennium.

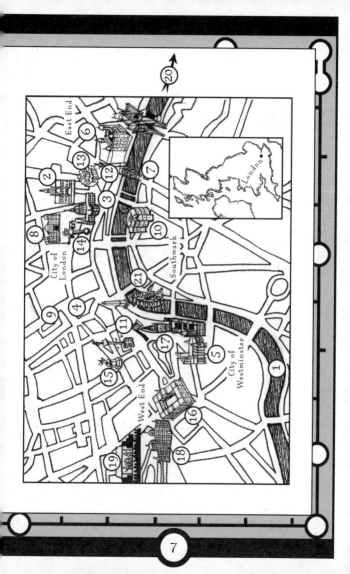

T he coat of arms of the City of London

The sword is said to be that of the brother of Cassivellaunus (see page 31). The Latin motto means 'Lord, guide us.'

INTRODUCTION

What makes London special?

London – big, isn't it? It's been that way for centuries: in the time of Queen Elizabeth I (1558–1603) the capital was 13 times larger than the second-biggest city in England, while even in the 1930s, one in five people in England and Wales lived in London.

To some, it's a monster that gobbles up everyone and everything: the crowds, the smells and the roar of traffic can overwhelm you. Yet London's size gives it energy – you only have to watch the mad dash of commuters during rush hour to feel the manic pulse of the city. That's partly because London has been re-energised again and again by waves of migrants, turning it into the great melting-pot it is today. Many of those who come are young, and though London is old, it is also a city of youth. Blink, and life will pass you by.

To others, the sprawling city is a glorious mess. London doesn't have the straight roads and neat numbered grid of New York or Chicago. That's because it spread out over hundreds of years, merging with scores of distinct villages as it grew, and gluing them together with bustling city streets. It's no surprise that London has not one but two centres – the City of London for trade and the City of Westminster for politics.

London sits right on top of an ancient Roman town, and every time a gleaming tower of glass and steel is built, part of the city's ancient heritage is revealed. The city is built up in heaps, with layers of history both cheek-by-jowl and buried under one another. It has been said that no stone ever leaves London –

it just gets reused, adding to the pile already there. As a result, much of its story is hidden, or at least not obvious at first glance.

Looking across the city from Parliament Hill (NW3), it's very hard to imagine Boudicca battling the Romans, the Saxon port of Ludenwic, or the lost rivers and streams that are now buried deep beneath the streets. All this buried history means our knowledge of the 'Big Smoke' is sometimes little more than a patchwork of loosely connected legends. Truth and lies mingle – but which is which?

The city's long and troubled past also means it's a bit like an old dog: lovable but rather scruffy, and more than a tad worn out. London has always been noisy, dirty and overcrowded. Though every once in a while a great fire or other disaster has reduced the city to ashes, somehow the mess and the chaos have always returned. If you think it's bad now, be thankful you avoided the Great Stink of 1858, when the whole city reeked like a giant toilet, or the 'pea-soupers' of the 1920s and 30s when the capital was wrapped in a thick, choking blanket of sooty fog.

When trains get cancelled, or you're stuck for what seems like an eternity in a dark Tube tunnel, don't be too harsh on the old place. Just ask: the city's inhabitants pride themselves on finding alternative routes under and over the city's twisting and turning streets. In fact, Londoners are nothing if not proud: it's not by chance that the popular name for them – Cockneys – began as an insult meaning 'cocky' or 'boastful'. Londoners are defiant, too, whether braving German bombs during the Blitz or taking to the streets in protest. Disorder and anarchy are as much a part of the capital's history as its beautiful squares and great monuments.

Brace yourself for all that London's very peculiar history has to offer, from the good and the bad to the downright ugly...

M
ost Londoners
speak English, a
language that is
used and understood the
world over.

* *Greetings, my friend! I noticed your father emerging from a public house yesterday evening.*

Curious place names

- **Bleeding Heart Yard,** Hatton Garden, EC1. In popular legend, the Hatton family made a pact with the Devil in order to achieve fame and fortune during the reign of Queen Elizabeth I. When the Devil came to claim his fee, he grabbed Lady Elizabeth Hatton's body and ripped her limb from limb, leaving only a bloody, still-beating heart!

- **Soho Square,** W1. Before the Great Fire of London in 1666, this part of the West End was open countryside. 'So-how!' was a cry used when hunting for hares, like the better-known 'Tally-ho!' Historians can't agree whether the cry gave its name to the place, or vice-versa.

- **Piccadilly,** W1. 'Piccadills' were pieces of material used to support the stiff collars, or ruffs, worn in Elizabethan times. When a rich tailor built a large house in the area in 1612, locals nicknamed it Piccadilly Hall after the trade that had made him rich. Though the big house was later demolished, the name lives on. Manchester, York and Bradford have streets named after it.

- **Pall Mall,** SW1. Named after the French game of *paille-mail*, first played here in the reign of King Charles I. Players whacked a ball towards a metal hoop, down a long, straight course.

- **Houndsditch,** EC3. Named after the ditch that ran beneath the city walls from the Tower to the old River Fleet – perhaps a dump for dead dogs in medieval times.

- **Threadneedle Street,** EC2. Its name may refer to the three needles that appear on the coat of arms of the Worshipful Company of Needlemakers, once based in this street.

- **Crutched Friars,** EC3. This street sits on the ruins of the priory of the Crossed Friars, founded in 1298. In Old English, the word for cross was *crouche*, which over the years got mispronounced as 'crutchèd'.

- **Frying Pan Alley,** E1. A frying pan was the sign of the many brassworkers and ironmongers who once had workshops along this lane.

- **Seven Sisters Road,** N15. The long road that runs from Holloway to Tottenham gets its name from a circle of trees. Some say they were planted by the family of Scots king Robert the Bruce, who lived nearby, in remembrance of his seven daughters. Others believe the site was once a sacred grove where ancient Britons worshipped.

- **Ha-Ha Road,** SE18. Not a joke, but named after a 'ha-ha', a sunken trench built in the late 18th century to stop cattle and sheep wandering onto the nearby Royal Artillery firing range at Woolwich.

Unlikely Londoners

London is made by the people who pass through, as well as those born in the capital.

- **Mahatma Gandhi** was a law student in London in the late 1880s, living at 20 Baron's Court Road, W14. He used to walk around London in search of vegetarian food (a rarity in those days). This got him into the habit of thinking on his feet and walking long distances. At the age of 61, he walked over 380 km to make salt from seawater – as a protest against British rule in India.

- **Vincent Van Gogh** spent some time in London as young man from 1873 to 1874, working for the art dealers Goupil & Cie. For a while he lived at 87 Hackford Road in Lambeth (SW9). He had his heart broken here, after falling madly in love with his landlady's daughter, Eugénie.

- **Voltaire.** This famous writer lived in London for three years after being expelled from France due to a quarrel with a nobleman, the Chevalier de Rohan. On one occasion he was chased through the streets by a mob, just for looking French. But the old fox won them over by telling them how much better it was to be English.

- **Pocahontas.** The Native American princess is credited with saving the life of Captain John

Smith, but she ended up marrying another Englishman, John Rolfe, and travelled with him to London in 1616. Here she became the talk of the town and even had her portrait painted. Sadly, she caught tuberculosis while in England and died a year later, aged just 22.

- **Cetewayo.** The proud Zulu king was allowed to travel to England only after his forces had been beaten. In 1879, his warriors had crushed the British forces in a surprise attack at the Battle of Isandlwana. Cetewayo met the British prime minister Gladstone and was celebrated in a music-hall song, which claimed he was something of a ladies' man.

- **Jules Léotard.** The French acrobat who inspired the famous song 'The Daring Young Man on the Flying Trapeze', Léotard first appeared at the Alhambra Theatre, Leicester Square, in May 1861. His trapeze show was a big hit at the time, but Léotard is best known today for the skin-tight one-piece garment that still bears his name. It was designed to show off his muscles!

- **Wolfgang Amadeus Mozart** arrived in London in April 1764 as part of a European tour organised by his father to make as much money as possible from the 8-year-old child prodigy. By the time they left, in July 1765, money was running low, and young Mozart was forced to perform keyboard tricks in local pubs.

London's 'villages'

No two London districts are alike:

- Royal **Kensington**, W8. Named after an Anglo-Saxon nobleman, Cynesige, the district became a home for royals in 1689 when William III moved into Kensington Palace. Queen Victoria was born here in 1819. In August 1997, thousands laid flowers at the palace gates after Princess Diana was killed in a car crash. Kensington is also home to one of London's best-kept secrets: the biggest roof garden in Europe, found on top of the Derry & Toms building, some 30 m above the street.

- Posh **Knightsbridge**, SW1. Named after a bridge across the Westbourne River on which two knights fought a duel, Knightsbridge is now home to many of the world's richest people. In 2008, a penthouse at One Hyde Park sold for for £100 million, at the time the most expensive flat in the world! Close by are two of London's most glamorous department stores, Harrods and Harvey Nichols.

- Artsy **Hampstead**, NW3. Despite its homely name, from the Old English for 'homestead', this village in north-west London has more millionaires than anywhere else in the UK and has long been a home for writers, composers, actors, artists and pop stars. Hampstead Heath, London's biggest ancient parkland, has fantastic views of the city.

- **Highgate**, City of the Dead (N6). On the north-eastern corner of Hampstead Heath, Highgate is home to one of London's finest cemeteries, the burial place of writers Karl Marx and George Eliot, and of murdered Russian spy Alexander Litvinenko.

- Radical **Stoke Newington**, N16. The 'new town on the wood' was once a small village outside London. By the mid-1800s it had merged with the ever-expanding city. In the 20th century, the area had a reputation for attracting radicals: the 'Stoke Newington 8' were arrested in 1971 for links to the Angry Brigade's bombing of banks and embassies.

- Dangerous **Blackheath**, SE3. The large heath in south-east London was used by Vikings as a camp from which to raid Kent. Later it was a rallying point for Wat Tyler's Peasants' Revolt of 1381. In the 17th century, it was a haunt for highwaymen as the famous Roman road of Watling Street crossed the heath on its way to the channel ports.

- Scientific **Greenwich**, SE10. Long linked with the Royal Navy, Greenwich is where time stands still – all time zones around the world are measured in hours before or after Greenwich Mean Time. Outside the Royal Observatory is a line marking the Prime Meridian between the Eastern and Western Hemispheres. Greenwich Palace was where gallant Sir Walter Raleigh spread his cloak to stop Queen Elizabeth I getting her feet wet.

Ten London firsts

1. **Champagne.** Taking advantage of sturdy English bottles that could withstand the extra pressure, scientist Christopher Merret invented the first sparkling wine in London in 1662 – 35 years before Dom Pérignon created his version in Champagne (though the French name stuck).

2. **TV.** On 26 January 1926, Scots engineer John Logie Baird gave the world's first demonstration of television before 50 scientists in an attic room in central London. A year earlier he had tried to give the *Daily Express* the scoop on his invention. The news editor told his staff: 'For God's sake, go down to reception and get rid of a lunatic who's down there. He says he's got a machine for seeing by wireless!'

3. **Pickle.** Bethnal Green landowner Sir Hugh Platt discovered that keeping freshly picked fruit in a vacuum made it last longer. Explorer and part-time pirate Sir Francis Drake was so impressed that he took Platt's bottled fruits on his next voyage.

4. **Curry house.** The first Indian-run eating place in London opened in 1809, off Portman Square. The Hindostanee Coffee-House was set up by ex-Indian Army man, Dean Mahomet. Today there are over 600 Indian restaurants in the capital.

5. **Vending machine.** 'The curious mathematical fountain' was set up in the Black Horse Tavern, Smithfield, at the end of the 17th century. It dispensed tea, coffee, whisky, cherry brandy and rum punch.

6. **Jigsaw puzzle.** John Spilsbury, a London engraver and mapmaker, made the first one in 1761 to teach children geography.

7. **Plastic.** The first man-made plastic, called Parkesine, was unveiled at the London International Exhibition by Alexander Parkes in 1862. Unlike rubber, this new material could be coloured or transparent, and could be moulded or carved to any shape.

8. **Derrick.** Tyburn hangman Thomas Derrick came up with a brilliant idea for a gallows that could support a dozen bodies at a time. His name is now used for any frame to lift heavy objects, such as the cranes on oil rigs.

9. **Roller skates.** A London instrument maker, Joseph Merlin, first showed off his wheeled boots at a party in 1760. He rode into the ballroom, playing the violin, then crashed into the mirror at the far end. Oops!

10. **Escalator.** One of the first escalators in the world was installed in Harrods in 1898, made of 224 pieces of tough leather linked together. Worried that customers might feel a bit giddy after their first ride, shop assistants gave out brandy and smelling salts.

G og and Magog: legendary giants outside Guildhall

These two wooden statues stood guard outside the entrance of the Guildhall (EC2) until they were destroyed in an air raid in 1940.

CHAPTER ONE

EARLY DAYS

from prehistory to the early Middle Ages

I f you like tall tales, there's no better man than 12th-century monk and all-round fibber Geoffrey of Monmouth. In his *History of the Kings of Britain*, Geoffrey traced the founding of London back to Brutus, the great-grandson of Aeneas.

In Roman legend, this Aeneas was a Trojan prince, one of the few survivors after the Greeks burnt Troy to the ground. He got into various scrapes in his travels around the Mediterranean, but he's best known for founding the great ancient city of Rome.

LONDON A VERY PECULIAR HISTORY

In Geoffrey's story, when Brutus lands in Britain it's inhabited by a race of giants. After wrestling two of them, Gog and Magog, into submission, Brutus chains them to the doors of his palace. Many years later, the brave hero is buried at the White Mound, where the Tower of London stands today.

Around 1,000 years later, King Lud, another shadowy figure, improves Brutus' palace by adding 'fair buildings, towers and walls', and names it Ludstown. Is this the origin of the word 'London'? Probably not, but no-one really knows for sure.[1]

In telling this story, Geoffrey probably hoped to make London sound as old as Rome but, to put it bluntly, it's total codswallop! However, the legend lives on: Gog and Magog are still regarded as the guardians of the City of London, and images of the two big brutes have been carried in the Lord Mayor's Show since the reign of King Henry V (1413–1422).

1. Another suggestion is the Celtic Llyd-don – 'fort by a stream'. A more exciting possibility is the Celtic word londos, meaning 'fierce', which suggests that Londoners have always been a rough crowd.

Top 10 prehistoric Londoners

1. Ancient crocodiles have been discovered in the clay below Islington.

2. Hippos once trampled over what is now Trafalgar Square.

3. In 1690, the remains of a woolly mammoth were found below modern-day King's Cross.

4. A well drilled below Queensway in 1888 uncovered teeth belonging to prehistoric sharks (known as 'tongue stones' because they look like dragons' tongues).

5. The remains of ancient brown bears were found in Woolwich.

6. A lion was found in Fleet Street in 1914. It had been dead for at least 10,000 years.

7. Giant beavers up to 2.5 m long once gnawed their way through trees south of Dartford.

8. Ancient rhinos once puffed their way across Greenwich.

9. Aurochs (giant wild cattle) were drowned near Ilford in a giant flood around 200,000 years ago.

10. Remains of Neanderthals have been found in Kent. These early humans probably hunted where London is now.

Swamp dwellers

The real story is a rather more soggy affair. Fifty million years ago, London was covered by the waters of a warm, shallow ocean. Its seabed created the soft clay that sits under the Thames Basin – the bowl-shaped valley that can still be seen from Canary Wharf Tower despite centuries of building. For hundreds of years, this clay has been made into London Stock, the famous brown and red bricks. It's also a great source of fossils.

Around 500,000 years ago, a giant early version of the River Thames flowed north-eastwards over much of what is now Suffolk. It got shoved into its current valley by an ice sheet some 50,000 years later. Much wider and wilder than it is today, the river was fed by countless streams and surrounded by forests, swamps and marshes. Animals came and went as the climate changed.

London was founded less than 2,000 years ago, but at least 500,000 years before this, odd groups of nomadic hunters and gatherers milled around the Thames Valley. The first to arrive were the Neanderthals. These early humans had shorter, chunkier bodies than us, and powerful arms and shoulders. Using wooden spears with flint heads, they hunted deer and mammoths by driving them into swamps or over cliffs.

The first humans to look anything like modern Londoners appeared some 40,000 years ago, and for 30,000 years they lived alongside the Neanderthals. They brought new tools and new hunting methods. When another ice age arrived around 22,000 BC, they headed south again. The Neanderthals vanished forever, for reasons we don't yet know.

You hunt, I'll gather.

Lost rivers

Several of London's rivers have disappeared underground over the centuries.

- **Walbrook.** Along with the Fleet, this provided a natural harbour in ancient times. Skulls found there in 1860 may belong to Roman soldiers slaughtered by Boudicca's bloodthirsty warriors.

- **Fleet.** Flowing from Hampstead Heath towards Blackfriars, this river was known for its awful pong, caused by bits of livestock flung from the slaughterhouses at the nearby Smithfield Market.

- **Effra.** Its name comes from the Celtic word for 'torrent'. Meeting the Thames near the MI6 building at Vauxhall, the Effra is now part of London's sewer system.

- **Tyburn.** This stream can be seen in the basement of Gray's Antiques in Davies Street (W1), where it forms a channel that's a home to goldfish.

- **Westbourne.** Rising in Hampstead and flowing through Knightsbridge, it was dammed in 1730 to help form the Serpentine lake in Hyde Park. The river is carried along a platform in Sloane Square Tube station through a great iron pipe.

Around 12,000 years ago, the return of a warmer climate convinced a few brave souls that the Thames Valley was a good place to settle down. Hunting camps near Uxbridge may have been used to ambush migrating herds of reindeer. Around 8,500 years ago, rising water levels turned Britain into an island once more and drowned low-lying areas along the Thames valley. The threat of flooding has never gone away (and could get a lot worse thanks to global warming).

That determined London spirit was already in evidence as wooden trackways were laid across marshy areas to link settlements and fields. New camps were built on higher ground, while clearings were made in the thick forest to lure animals into the open.

By 3500 BC, some groups were growing their own crops, and the remains of a wooden house discovered near Runnymede Bridge date back to the same period. We know a lot about these early inhabitants from the piles of rubbish they left – a bad habit still shared by Londoners today.

In the Bronze Age, from 2300 to 700 BC, the Thames was still a huge barrier dividing north and south. It was not so much a single river as a group of channels running through mudflats and past small islands.[2] The river was the home of gods and spirits worshipped by the people living along its banks, and it has inspired legends and lore ever since.

Already London seems to have been a good place to do business. Fragments of pots, bowls and tools have been found all over the city, many close to the twin hills of Cornhill and Ludgate Hill. When the Celts arrived in Britain, some time after 500 BC, there was already a brisk trade in slaves, corn and metal goods with merchants from across Europe. The newcomers, though small in number, made a big impact: they showed the locals how to make weapons and tools from iron, which was much tougher than bronze. Some London street names come from Celtic words, such as Maiden Lane and Ingal Road; Herne Hill may be named after the Celtic god of hunting.

2. When Westminster Abbey was first built in the 12th century, it sat on Thorney Island, which lay between two branches of the river Tyburn where it joined the Thames.

Welcome to Londinium

If an ancient Briton ever asked 'What have the Romans done for us?' a one-word retort could have been: 'Londinium' (the Roman word for London). When Julius Caesar's expedition reached the Thames Valley in 55–54 BC it found a glorified swamp with a few small settlements and farmsteads. The only town worthy of note was a camp about 40 km north of the river, which belonged to local chieftain Cassivellaunus.

With nothing to write home about, Caesar headed off, never to return. If we believe Caesar, his invasion force included 800 ships, 5 legions and 2,000 cavalrymen. It was the largest naval landing in the history of the world until D-Day in 1944. All in all, he must have been rather disappointed!

The Romans were back again in AD 43, this time to stay. According to the Roman historian Cassius Dio, they lost a few soldiers in the swamps of the Thames Valley but quickly swatted away the locals. The Romans were great builders, and with a bit of TLC and a lot of blood, sweat and tears, they soon turned the wooden frontier settlement into a true capital with some 25,000 inhabitants.

Not everyone admired the new settlers. In AD 60 the Iceni tribe, based in East Anglia, revolted after the Romans whipped their queen, Boudicca, and sold some of them into slavery. Exacting a terrible revenge, they put 30,000 Londoners to the sword and burnt the city to the ground – the first of many devastating fires. The blaze is forever marked by a bright red layer of soil some 4 metres below today's streets.

The Roman governor regrouped his forces and eventually defeated Boudicca, who poisoned herself to avoid capture. According to one far-fetched story, her body lies buried below platform 10 at King's Cross Station, supposedly the site of her last battle against the Romans. (In reality this was somewhere in the Midlands.) Near the Houses of Parliament, a giant bronze statue of Boudicca in her war chariot now stands guard over the city she burnt to the ground.

Fortunately, London has always found a way to rise from the ashes. It took 20 years to recover from the destruction, but the city was thriving again by AD 100. For 300 years, the new Londinium was the largest city in Britannia. It had a fort where the Barbican Centre is now, an amphitheatre (now buried below the Guildhall) and public bath houses. Crucially, the Romans also built a bridge across the Thames.[3] The river faced the mighty Rhine, which was the gateway to the heart of Europe. With its inland seaport and waterways, the city was well placed for lucrative trade with the rest of the sprawling Roman empire.[4]

Boudicca

Britain's first Iron Lady

3. 'Thames' is one of the oldest place names still in use in Britain: it was given the name Tamesis by Julius Caesar.
4. In 1962 a Roman shipwreck was discovered in the Thames, dating from around AD 150.

The new city grew around the bridge, which was also the hub for half a dozen roads leading to the rest of the country. The Romans ran the whole province from London, which naturally became a centre for administration and law as well as trade. The governor had a large mansion where Cannon Street is today. The mysterious London Stone, which has been a noted landmark since the 11th century, may have been the military milestone from which distances were measured on all Roman roads in Britain. One old yarn says it's linked to Brutus, the legendary founder of London – while the stone is safe, London will flourish.[5]

What was Roman London like? For the only time in its history, it had a neat grid of streets and a giant central market-place, or *forum*, that was four times the size of Trafalgar Square. This contained a colossal basilica (a hall for public meetings) and was surrounded by temples and council offices. Tombstones with German and Greek names show that it was

5. *The London Stone had a narrow escape in 1940 when a German bomb flattened the Church of St Swithin's across the road, where the stone was kept at the time. It now stands next to the modern Bank of China, 11 Cannon St.*

already a home for people from all corners of the Empire.[6] Roman fashions were mixed and matched with native clothes such as woollen leggings (better suited to the British climate!) to create a funky look unique to Londinium.

Roman Londoners enjoyed feasts, gambling and music at home, or going to the public baths or amphitheatre. Here they watched executions, boxing and – on rare occasions – gladiator shows. There may have been a circus for chariot racing, just south of St Paul's, though this probably isn't linked to Knightrider Street just a short walk away! When a favour from heaven was needed, the Romans had all the bases covered: there were temples and shrines throughout the city, dedicated to Celtic and Eastern deities as well as Roman gods such as Jupiter.

One section of the Roman city wall – with a few medieval patches – can still be seen by Trinity Place, just north of the Tower of London.

6. *The body of a Roman woman found in Spitalfields shows the cosmopolitan nature of Roman London. DNA tests show that she was from Italy or Spain, and her body was found alongside a piece of fabric embroidered with silk thread from China.*

London Bridge lore

- The medieval bridge had 19 small arches and a drawbridge with a gatehouse at the southern end. The narrow arches created fierce rapids below the bridge, and many drowned trying to shoot the rapids.

- During Jack Cade's rebellion in 1450, a pitched battle was fought on the bridge.

- The head of Scots rebel William Wallace was the first to appear on the gate, in 1305, starting a grisly tradition that lasted another 355 years.

- In one legend, a pedlar (door-to-door salesman) from Swaffham in Norfolk dreams that if he goes to the bridge, good news will follow. After kicking his heels for several hours, the pedlar is finally approached by a curious shopkeeper, who tells him his own dream of finding a great treasure under an oak tree – in Swaffham! Needless to say, the pedlar heads back home, digs under the tree and hey presto, finds a pot of gold.

- London Bridge is also home to Doggett's boat race, which takes place on or near 1 August. It was started by a popular London actor, Thomas Doggett, in 1714 and has been run every year since (except during the Second World War). The winners march in bright red coats in the Lord Mayor's parade.

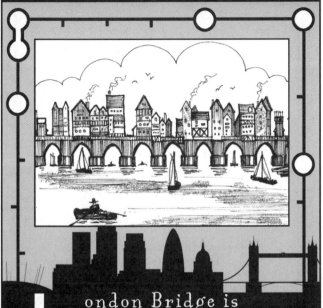

London Bridge is falling – under the hammer!

The medieval London Bridge (above) was replaced by John Rennie's design in 1831. In 1968, Rennie's bridge was sold to American businessman Robert P. McCulloch for $2.5 million. It was taken apart piece by piece and rebuilt at Lake Havasu City, Arizona. There is absolutely no truth in the rumour that McCulloch thought he was buying the more spectacular Tower Bridge.

Some unusual church names

- **St Clement Danes,** WC2. The first church on the site was built by Danish Vikings; these seafaring folk naturally dedicated it to St Clement, the patron saint of mariners. King Harold Harefoot is said to have been buried here in 1040 after his body was dug up from its original tomb and flung into the Thames marshes by his brother Cnut the Hardy.

- **St Magnus the Martyr,** EC3. This church is dedicated to Magnus Erlendsson, the peace-loving Norwegian Earl of Orkney who refused to take part in Viking raids and was killed by his cousin Haakon in 1116.

- **St Andrew-by-the-Wardrobe,** EC4. In 1361, Edward III moved his Royal Wardrobe (a storehouse for arms and clothing) from the Tower of London to just north of the church.

- **St James Garlickhythe,** EC4. The name refers to the nearby landing place, or *hythe*, where garlic was sold in medieval times. Until recently, visitors could see a mummified body, nicknamed Jimmy Garlic, in a cupboard at the back of the church.

- **St Andrew Undershaft,** EC3. A survivor of the Great Fire of 1666, this is named after a towering maypole put up outside the church in the 15th century. In 1517, a mob of city apprentices rioted against foreigners during 'Evil May Day'. The maypole was taken down and never used again.

Anglo-Saxon London

The Romans shipped out at the end of the 5th century, partly because of trouble back home – the beastly Goths sacked Rome in AD 410. For Londoners there were other invaders lurking nearby: raids by Angles and Saxons from the Continent were on the up, and within a generation the Roman way of life had disappeared. By 470, London was virtually abandoned.

Slowly, however, a new London emerged from the shadows. In AD 597 a group of Christian missionaries arrived to breathe life back into the old city. St Pancras (NW1), one of the first Christian churches in Britain, may have been built by St Augustine himself, the founder of the English Church.

Writing in 730, the historian Bede describes London as a big market town. The old city was left in ruins while a new town, Ludenwic, grew up where Covent Garden and the Strand are today.[7] Home to a few hundred people,

7. *A strand is literally a beach on the river, a natural place for the Saxons to load and unload their ships.*

this bustling town had workshops and markets, its own cathedral church, and a king's palace (near Wood St, EC2).

The new generation of Londoners had only just got into the swing of things when the Vikings turned up and spoilt the party. In 842 the Danes were beaten back by the plucky Londoners, but they returned nine years later with a fleet of 350 ships and sacked the city. Forty years later, the Saxons fought back under King Alfred the Great. After a three-year siege they recaptured the city in 886. Since the Vikings still held sway over much of eastern and northern England, the Anglo-Saxons who remained decided it was far safer to re-start the city inside the Roman walls.

The process of rebuilding probably took place over a long time, but King Alfred certainly gave the city a boost by building new roads and quays and restoring the old walls.

Though Londoners were now (fairly) safe from the Vikings, the 10th century brought other problems – there was a great fire in 961, followed by a plague and then another fire 20 years later. Things took another turn for the worse when the Danes arrived in force under King Sweyn Forkbeard, but the Saxon king Aethelred found an unlikely ally in the Norwegian prince Olaf.

The famous Nursery rhyme 'London Bridge is falling down' may echo the legend that Olaf got his ships to pull the wooden bridge into the Thames, helped by the strong tides. The Danes were stopped in their tracks, and grateful Londoners named six churches after Olaf.[8]

Around the same time, a group of Danish traders settled outside the walls near the site of the old Saxon town, marked today by the Church of St Clement Danes (WC2). Danes and Saxons now lived side by side, and the city absorbed the newcomers as it was to do time and again in the centuries that followed.

London already had its own army and the right to govern itself. It also became a centre of royal power when the Anglo-Saxon king Edward the Confessor built a new palace at

8. Including St Olave's in Hart St (EC3), where Samuel Pepys used to ogle ladies through a telescope when he got bored.

Westminster – just a stone's throw from his
new abbey, where all kings and queens of
England have been crowned ever since.

London now replaced Winchester as the
principal town of England. Unusually, the city
had two centres: a trading centre on the site of
the old Roman city, and a political centre at
Westminster, which in those days was little
more than an island connected by a single
road from Charing Cross.

The stormin' Normans

When Edward the Confessor died in 1066,
he left no heirs, kicking off a three-way battle
for the English crown between Harold
Godwinson, an Anglo-Saxon noble; Harald
Hardrada, King of Norway; and William,
Duke of Normandy. Hardrada of Norway
struck first and was beaten by Harold
Godwinson, who then rushed south to face
William's forces at the Battle of Hastings.

Harold got an arrow in the eye and was cut
down by Norman knights. The rest, as they
say, is history. William marched on London,

but after crushing an English force at Southwark, he was unable to storm London Bridge. Heading north, he finally battered the Saxons into submission and was crowned king at Westminster Abbey on 25 December 1066.

William, now 'the Conqueror', let Londoners know who was boss by building three military camps in London. One eventually became the Tower of London, which was evermore seen by Londoners as a symbol of oppression rather than defence.

The Tower

Caw!

William soon worked out that the city was the key to governing the rest of England. He kept the wealthy merchants happy by allowing them to keep their ancient laws and freedoms in return for paying taxes. He and his successors turned London into a true capital. They began the great process of building and rebuilding that continues today.

A ring of monasteries, nunneries, priories and hospitals grew up outside the walls of the old Roman city, and in 1176 the first stone bridge was built across the Thames. The Normans also used another great fire in 1087 as an excuse to build a new cathedral, St Paul's, which dominated London's skyline for nearly 600 years. William II started work on the great hall at Westminster, and the first Guildhall was built in 1127.[9]

The Norman Conquest of 1066 brought new inhabitants from northern France, including many Jews who set up businesses in the

9. This was where the Lord Mayor and the ruling merchant class held court and fine-tuned the laws that helped create London's wealth. Nearly 900 years later, it is still home to the council that runs the City of London (the old walled city, now the home of the banking sector).

Cheapside area. Many were moneylenders who helped to finance the growing city. Although they were supposed to be under the king's protection, 30 Jewish merchants were massacred in 1189 after the coronation of Richard I.

The arrival of Flemish and French cloth workers also gave a huge boost to London, which became a centre for the European wool trade. The second half of the 12th century was a time of prosperity and growth. The workers began to form clubs, or guilds, beginning with the weavers in 1130. Within 50 years there were 20 guilds, including goldsmiths, pepperers (the spice trade), clothworkers and butchers.

Something of a late developer, London was now shaping up into the metropolis we might recognise today. The built-up areas remained within the old Roman walls, and Londoners entered and left the city through seven gates. None survive, but their names live on: Ludgate, Newgate, Aldersgate, Cripplegate, Moorgate, Bishopsgate and Aldgate.

Legends of the Tower

The White Tower was built in 1078 by William the Conqueror to control the city of London. It has been used as a fortress, a palace and a prison. Famous prisoners include:

- King Henry VI, murdered here in 1471.

- The Princes in the Tower (King Edward V and his brother Richard of Shrewsbury). In popular legend their wicked uncle, later Richard III, locked them in the Tower and had them smothered to death with pillows.

- Henry VIII's second wife, Anne Boleyn, beheaded with a single stroke of the axe in 1536, just north of the White Tower. Henry's fifth wife, Catherine Howard, got the chop just six years later.

- Sir Walter Raleigh was a prisoner for 13 years (1603-1616), though he lived in comfort with his wife and children.

- Guy Fawkes, famous for his part in the Gunpowder Plot, was questioned (but not executed) at the Tower.

- Rudolf Hess, deputy leader of the Nazi Party, was held in the Tower in May 1941.

- East End gangsters the Kray twins were among the last prisoners to be held here, in 1952, for running away from the army.

Long before the Normans got to work, the hill the tower stands on, known as the White Mount, was already a sacred place. As the giant warrior Brân lay dying, he asked friends to chop off his head and bury it on the site of the Tower, with his face towards France. Supposedly, England will be safe as long as Brân's head remains...

Brân's bird was the raven, and traditionally six ravens are on duty at the Tower, with others in reserve. They are fed on raw meat and biscuits soaked in blood, with the occasional treat of rabbit which they eat fur and all. The birds are great mimics: one can bark like a dog, while another says 'Hello' in a spookily deep voice.

For about 600 years, the Tower housed a menagerie (zoo). The mini-zoo was open to the public in the 18th century; it cost three halfpence, but you got in for free if you brought along a cat or dog to feed to the lions.

Two torture devices used in the Tower were the 'scavenger's daughter', which squashed the poor victim into a ball, and the rack (nicknamed the 'Duke of Exeter's daughter' after its inventor), which stretched them out again.

A curfew bell is rung every night to remind residents to put out their candles.

Legend has it that grass cannot grow in the Outer Ward because so much blood has been spilt there.

Bring out your dead! The plague was a regular visitor to London from the 14th century to the 17th.

CHAPTER TWO

GROWING PAINS

Medieval, Tudor and Stuart London

By the 13th century, London already had a population of 80,000, making it one of the largest cities in Europe. It was also richer than the next nine towns in England put together. Though its streets aren't paved with gold, the city has always been built on money.[1]

With money came power, and London made the most of the rivalry between Richard I and his brother John, who ruled England while

1. *The two griffins on the south entrance to today's London Bridge are mythical guardians of gold mines and buried treasure.*

Richard was away on Crusade.[2] To win over the wealthy merchants of London, John agreed in 1191 to let them govern themselves. Foolishly, he then tried to bleed them dry with a series of new taxes. When the king clashed with his barons, the city backed the rebels and opened its gates to them. The mayor of London was among those who forced John to sign Magna Carta in 1215 – the first time anyone had set a limit on the king's power.[3]

The power games didn't end there. In 1216, five Londoners paid the French prince Louis 1,000 marks to replace John. When John suddenly died, they agreed to support Henry III, John's son. Henry ruled London directly for 13 years, though he was the last king to do so. Later kings were happy to give the City of London its independence – as long as they got paid. From now on, whenever a king needed money, he came cap in hand to the City.

2. Richard was unpopular for the heavy taxes he created to pay for his Crusade. Londoners were even less happy paying his ransom in 1194, when he was held prisoner by the French king Henry VI – especially after Richard said, 'I'd sell London if I could find a buyer.'
3. Magna Carta, or the Great Charter, was signed at Runnymede, a meadow that runs alongside the Thames about 30 km west of London. You can see a copy of this momentous document for yourself in the British Museum in Great Russell St (WC2).

While business was booming, the leading merchants, barons and churchmen bought large courtyard houses in London, many along the Strand. This road connected the City to the palace at Westminster, allowing them to cosy up to the king whenever possible. There was big money to be made at court, and London was the place to make your millions.

London was home to England's first parliament in the 13th century, as well as the law courts, and the Exchequer that organised the royal finances. It was also a great religious centre.[4] The Church was London's biggest landowner and its biggest employer. As well as abbeys, monasteries and hospitals, the capital had 100 churches within its walls, more than any other city in Europe.

By the early 12th century the capital had its own town hall, the Guildhall, which was built on the ruins of the Roman amphitheatre. The first stone bridge was built in 1176, although it was often clogged, and most people crossed the river using ferries.

4. London's patron saint was Bishop Erkenwald, the centre of a cult in which old men were wheeled around the city on a cart.

famous chimes

Before the arrival of the motor car, the bells of London churches could be heard many miles away. The famous rhyme 'Oranges and Lemons' celebrates their chimes while reflecting daily life in the capital:

- 'Oranges and Lemons/Say the bells of St Clement's' - Citrus fruit was unloaded at a nearby quay.

- 'Bullseyes and targets/Say the bells of St Margaret's' - Calling all Robin Hoods: there's an archery field just around the corner.

- 'Brickbats and tiles/Say the bells of St Giles' - London's builders were at it again.

- 'Pancakes and fritters/Say the bells of St Peter's' - Follow the chimes for a slap-up meal.

- 'You owe me five farthings/Say the bells of St Martin's' - Need a loan? Moneylenders traded near this church.

Medieval fashion victims

Londoners did their best to copy the very latest fashions at court.

Around 1190, London had its first mayor, Henry Fitz Aylwin – though real power lay in the hands of the aldermen, the members of the city council. The craft guilds, known today as the Livery Companies, continued to grow. Their members wore a distinctive uniform and had the freedom of the city. The problems confronting the first Mayor of London are still around 800 years later:

- providing clean water
- encouraging trade
- protecting against fire
- getting rid of the rubbish.

London was divided into areas known as 'wards', each responsible for its own water, policing, paving, sewers and lighting. Street-cleaners cleared up rubbish and the dung from pigs and other animals that roamed the streets. Lead pipes were used to bring spring water into the city from 5 km away – one of the first water systems in medieval Europe.

Yet the capital was already a filthy slum. Soot, dust and mud covered everything, and the smells of dung mingled with the stink from the tanneries and the fish markets. Market stalls ran along the middle of the street, forcing pedestrians to squeeze past on either side.

Medieval London may sound a colourful, energetic place to live, but it was also full of danger, from drownings and stabbings to slips and falls. Fire was a constant threat in the narrow streets. Riots were two a penny, and the craft guilds fought each other in pitched battles. Even the sons of rich folk got together in gangs to beat up passers-by. Mercifully, the city kept a close eye on its citizens, and no-one was allowed out after 9 p.m. in summer.

With the dirt came disease, especially the bubonic plague and the 'sweating sickness'. In poorer areas, Londoners were lucky to live to 30. By the end of the Middle Ages, London had at least 12 hospitals. They were badly needed, as many Londoners were ill-fed and lived in shacks. Hundreds died of starvation every year, especially in years when the harvest failed. In 1338, 'Poor people ate cats and horses and hounds . . . and stole children and ate them.' Fifty people were trampled to death when the monks of Blackfriars priory handed out free food to a ravenous crowd.

My Lord Mayor

Since 1190, the Lord Mayor has represented the businesses and the people of the City of London, the area once enclosed by the city walls. He is elected by a show of hands among the Livery Companies (see page 54), and the result is celebrated by the Lord Mayor's Show. This is still one of the biggest annual events in London – the Lord Mayor travels in a horse-drawn coach dating from 1757, and the event can involve over 250 vehicles and 70 floats.

- **Richard Whittington** was a merchant who funded public works in poor parts of London. Rather dull in real life, somehow he inspired the pantomime story of Dick Whittington, in which a poor orphan makes his way to London after hearing that the streets are paved with gold. Meeting with little success, the boy heads out of the city. Whilst climbing Highgate Hill, he hears the bells of London telling him to 'turn again'. In one version, Dick makes his fortune thanks to the rat-catching abilities of his trusty cat.

- **Mayor William Walworth** is famous for drawing his sword and fatally wounding the leader of the Peasants' Revolt, Wat Tyler, at Smithfield in 1381.

- **Sir Thomas Bludworth** goes down in history as the Lord Mayor who, when first told of the Great Fire of London, said, 'A woman might piss it out' as he snuggled back under the sheets. As the fire grew worse he refused to pull down houses in its path. This might have stopped the blaze from spreading so far and burning four-fifths of the city to the ground.

- As a young man, **Mayor John Wilkes** foolishly made an enemy of the famous painter William Hogarth. Hogarth drew a hideous caricature of Wilkes, making fun of his crossed eyes. Despite this, the silver-tongued Wilkes could supposedly charm any woman in a matter of minutes.

Shepherd's delight

The first freedom of the City of London was granted in 1237. In those days it meant a great deal: you were no longer under the thumb of your feudal lord. Freemen were given a parchment inside a wooden box that worked a bit like a passport. Today, around 1,800 people a year become freemen (the term is used for women and men). Some of the traditional rights still remain. In theory, freemen can:

- herd sheep over London Bridge (this was originally to do with avoiding tolls)
- walk around the City with a drawn sword
- get married in St Paul's
- be drunk and disorderly without fear of arrest
- if sentenced to hanging, insist on a silk rope!

The Big Stink

London may be a bit dirty and smelly now, but the stench of days gone by doesn't bear thinking about:

- Famous for their plumbing, the Romans saw a trip to the toilet as a chance for a good natter with friends and family. Instead of paper, the poor used a sponge on a short wooden handle, while the rich tickled themselves clean with ostrich feathers.

- The Saxons had little time for luxuries. They used pots or deep holes in the ground. By medieval times, London was an open sewer. Toilets called *garderobes* emptied straight into the streets or the Thames.

- In the 1400s, Lord Mayor Dick Whittington paid for a giant public lavatory, nicknamed 'Whittington's Longhouse', that could seat 100 people.

- Henry VIII's courtiers at Hampton Court shared a mass toilet with 28 seats on two levels. The royal loos were cleaned by a team of 'gong scourers' – boys small enough to crawl along the drains.

- Even in the 1800s, ordinary people flung the contents of their pots in the street – they didn't realise that with sewage came deadly diseases such as typhoid and cholera.

- There are no prizes for guessing the origins of streets such as Pissing Lane, Dunghill Lane, Pudding Lane and Sherborne Lane (originally 'Shiteburn' Lane).

- A heatwave in 1858 caused the famous 'Big Stink': London reeked like a giant toilet. Enough was enough. The government finally got around to building a modern sewer system, which was finished in 1865, and people stopped dying of typhoid and cholera.

- In late Victorian times, London was famous for its magnificent toilets, called 'halting stations'. They cost a penny to use, giving us the expression 'spending a penny'.

During the 14th century, one disaster followed another in quick succession: famines, a long and destructive war with France, and then to cap it all, in 1348, rats on ships from Europe brought the Black Death. This bubonic plague wiped out half of all Londoners in just 18 months, and it took 150 years for the population to recover. The plague wasn't all bad, though: trade continued to grow, and some survivors did very well from an unexpected inheritance.

The Peasants' Revolt

In the short term, fewer workers led to higher wages, but kings, nobles and knights continued to stomp on the poor at every opportunity. The century had already seen its fair share of riots and massacres when King Richard II come up with a bright idea: a tax that was the same for a poor peasant as it was for a rich baron. This was the final straw, and in June 1381 tens of thousands of peasants marched in protest on London.

Always up for a fight, the London mob joined in. The rebels stormed the Tower of London and lopped the heads off the Lord Chancellor and the Lord Treasurer. Richard II arranged to meet the rebel leader, Wat Tyler, the next day at Smithfield. When Tyler was cut down (Lord Mayor William Walworth struck the first blow), the 14-year-old king bravely rode toward the rebel army and announced: 'You shall have no captain but me.' He'd won enough time to raise an army, and the rebel leaders were soon arrested and executed.

Legal London

- The Inns of Court are a warren of cloisters, courtyards and passageways set amongst some of the best gardens in London.

- Every barrister in England must belong to one of the surviving four Inns (so-called because they they were originally more like hotels than offices): Gray's Inn, Lincoln's Inn and the Inner and Middle Temples. Lincoln's Inn is perhaps the oldest, dating back to 1422. It can claim 15 prime ministers among its former members.

- In the 14th century, lawyers were banned from setting up their own college in the City of London. In typical fashion, they simply set up shop outside the city walls.

- Over the years, there were regular clashes with the City authorities. When a fire broke out and no help came from the City, the lawyers are said to have put it out with wine and beer from their own cellars.

Troubled times

For 30 years in the late 15th century, the noble houses of Lancaster and York slugged it out in the Wars of the Roses. Henry Tudor emerged as the victor and was crowned Henry VII in 1485, at a time when London was growing in wealth and stature. Seven years later, Christopher Columbus accidentally sailed into the Bahamas, opening up the New World. Spotting a business opportunity, Henry backed explorer John Cabot's expedition, which in 1497 was the first to land in North America. London's merchants must have licked their lips at the news that there was a whole new continent to trade with!

Henry Tudor's son, Henry VIII, however, cast an even bigger shadow over London. He broke from the Catholic Church when the Pope refused to divorce him from his first wife, Catherine of Aragon. His solution was simple but devastating: he made himself head of the new Church of England and went ahead and married a second wife, Anne Boleyn. As England was now Protestant, Henry 'dissolved' the monasteries around 1532, which is a polite way of saying that he tore them down, robbed their treasures and flogged off their lands.

The face of medieval London was transformed. Henry VIII grabbed large chunks of land to hunt on – what is now Hyde Park, Regent's Park and Richmond Park. Many religious houses vanished altogether, leaving only their names.[5] The Church of the Crutched Friars became a carpenter's workshop; a tavern was built on the remains of St Martin's le Grand (EC1). Even in posh areas, many buildings were simply left in ruins. But many former monasteries became sites for shiny new mansions. Henry himself built a string of new palaces.

> I have 60 assorted houses and palaces. It's nice to have a change of scene occasionally.

5. For example, Blackfriars bridge (EC4) is named after Blackfriars priory, home to Dominican friars who wore black habits.

Royal residences

- **Palace of Westminster** (SW1). Edward the Confessor's palace, built around 1045–1050, was the main residence of the kings of England until 1512. The first Parliament of England met here in 1295, as has every parliament since. Though most of the original building burned down in 1834, Westminster Hall and the Jewel Tower survive.

- **Hampton Court** (KT8) was given to Henry VIII by Cardinal Wolsey in 1528, in a vain attempt to stay in favour. It became Henry's chief court. The kitchens were built to feed 1,000 people.

- **Bridewell** (EC4), another of Henry VIII's palaces, became a refuge for the homeless in 1556, and then a prison, workhouse and hospital. The idea was that hard labour would reform petty criminals and those with a drink problem. Conditions were so appalling that 'bridewell' became a byword for harsh treatment – it's still used as a nickname for police stations or cells. The Crown Plaza Hotel stands on the site today.

- **Whitehall** (SW1). Tudor and Stuart monarchs held court in this sprawling palace-cum-leisure complex (the largest in Europe) that combined 1,500 rooms with tennis courts, a bowling alley, a pit for cockfighting and a tiltyard for jousting. Most of the palace burned down in 1698, though the great

Banqueting Hall survives. King Charles I was executed outside the palace in 1649.

- **St James's Palace** (SW1). Built for Henry VIII in 1536 on the site of a leper hospital, St James's became the king's official residence after Whitehall burned down. Queen Anne gave birth to nearly all of her 17 children here. The surviving gatehouse remains one of London's most famous Tudor landmarks.

- **Kensington Palace** (W8). William III, who suffered from asthma, moved into Kensington Palace in the late 17th century to get away from the city smoke, when Kensington was a village surrounded by open fields. It was the main royal residence until the death of George II in 1760.

- **Kew Palace** (Richmond, TW7). Three palaces have been built at Kew, but the doll's house of a palace that survives today was the home of George III and his family from 1729 to 1818. When Queen Victoria came to the throne she gave the gardens to the people, creating the famous Royal Botanic Gardens.

- **Buckingham Palace** (SW1) sits where James I once had a mulberry garden. It's been the official London home of the British monarch since 1837. When the Queen is in residence the Royal Standard flies from the flagpole. The palace has the largest private gardens in London, the setting for the 8,000 or so guests invited to Royal Garden Parties each summer.

Henry's daughter, 'Bloody Mary', tried to steer the country back to Catholicism, burning over 200 Protestants at Smithfield (EC1) in just four years (1554–1558). When her sister Elizabeth I came to the throne, hundreds more believers died on the gallows at Tyburn. This time they were Catholics, now blamed by Londoners for every plot or disaster.

After this bloody beginning, Elizabeth's 45-year reign (1558–1603) was a golden age. England became a naval superpower, boosted by the victory over the Spanish Armada in 1588. With English explorers and pirates trading and raiding across the globe, London became a hot place to do a deal – helped by the creation of the Royal Exchange in 1566, where bankers and merchants could meet in comfort. London's population grew in leaps and bounds, despite plagues and other catastrophes:

- 1500: 75,000 people in London
- 1580: 150,000
- 1660: 500,000.

The city's growing reputation attracted more migrants, mainly from France and Holland.[6] Venetian glassmakers, Dutch tilers and Italian armourers (who set up the Royal Armoury) all brought specialist skills. When William Caxton set up the first printing press in Westminster in 1476, a new industry was born. By the 16th century, London was the centre of the English book trade, based around St Paul's Cathedral.

Elizabeth's reign also saw the rise of the merchant adventurers who dealt in goods from the new colonies in America and India, such as tobacco, sugar and pepper. By 1700 the global market was in full swing, and goods from Asia and the Americas accounted for a third of all trade into London.

The city was bursting at the seams. Property prices soared and new streets sprang up in the surrounding fields. London exploded west along the Strand, east along Whitechapel High Street, north to Clerkenwell, and south beyond Southwark.

6. In the mid-17th century, Dutch immigrants were clustered in Broad St and the French around Threadneedle St. In the 1640s Cromwell allowed Jews to return to London; they were now based around Aldgate.

Tudor Londoners didn't live in flats: every house had its own front door, even if it only opened out into a filthy back alleyway. Thousands were crammed into flimsy houses; poor families lived in one or two rooms, or even in cellars. The streets were full of pits and potholes. The craze for one-horse Hackney coaches (1625) and sedan chairs (1634) only added to the city's traffic problems.

The chaotic energy of Elizabethan London inspired some of England's finest ever playwrights. Shakespeare, Marlowe and Ben Jonson breathed new life into the English language while putting bums on seats. Outdoor playhouses such as the Rose (1587), Globe (1599) and Hope (1613) were banned from the old city, so they were built alongside the brothels, taverns and bearpits of Southwark, London's 'naughty' quarter.

1598 saw the publication of the first guidebook and map of London, *A Survey of London* by John Stow.[7] London was already a magnet for tourists.

7. In the church of St Andrew Undershaft there's still a ceremony in his honour: each year the Lord Mayor places a new red quill into his statue's hand.

The play was the thing in Elizabethan London.

A grisly end

The death penalty was in force in England until the second half of the 20th century – and the methods used could be very imaginative:

- In 1532, it took two hours to boil Richard Rose to death after he was convicted of killing at least 16 people.

- When the Duke of Monmouth was beheaded in 1685, executioner Jack Ketch took eight swings of the axe and still had to hack through the final strands with a knife.

- The last criminals beheaded in public in London were the Cato Street Conspirators in 1820, after they had been hanged. The executioner held up each head but dropped one, leading to cries of 'Butterfingers!'

- During the 18th century the main arch in Temple Bar (the western limit of the City of London) was used to display the heads of traitors. When the Rye House plotters got the chop in 1683, telescopes were hired out so spectators could see the heads clearly!

- From 1196 to 1783, Tyburn was *the* place for hangings. Crowds cheered or jeered as the condemned were brought by cart from Newgate prison. The cart was parked below the hanging tree, a noose placed around each victim's neck, and the horses kicked into action.

- Hangings were often botched, so family and friends tugged on their loved ones' feet to give them a quick death. The bodies of the hanged were said to cure all manner of diseases. In the 17th century, a severed hand could fetch 10 guineas (£10.50).

- Those convicted of witchcraft were hanged. Burning at the stake was used to punish those guilty of treason, which included forging coins or murdering your husband. Prisoners were usually strangled or hanged before the flames were lit, but Protestants executed by Mary I were literally burnt to death, a slow and excruciatingly painful end.

- The most gruesome punishment was reserved for traitors and for rebels such as William Wallace, who led the Scots in a revolt against English rule. Following his trial in 1305, Wallace was stripped and dragged through the streets behind a horse. At Smithfield he was:

  1. **hung**
  2. **drawn** (Still alive, his bowels were ripped out and burnt in front of him.)
  3. **quartered** (He was beheaded and his body cut into four parts.)

  Wallace's head was dipped in tar, then placed on a pike on London Bridge.

- In 1605, sneaky Guy Fawkes avoided drawing and quartering by jumping from the gallows and breaking his neck.

Tourist attractions included the Tower, St Paul's, London Bridge, Hyde Park, Westminster, and the theatres on the South Bank. Visitors then headed for London's famed eating-houses to sample such delicacies as Lambeth ale, Islington cheesecake, gingerbread from Fleet Lane, and the pancakes of Rosemary Lane. How little has changed!

When Elizabeth died in 1603, the crown passed to her cousin, James I. James incited the wrath of Guy Fawkes, Robert Catesby and other Catholic conspirators who plotted to blow up Parliament (with James inside) on 5 November 1605. Londoners were encouraged to celebrate the King's narrow escape by lighting bonfires in the city, starting a tradition that has persisted ever since.

When James's son Charles I came to the thone in 1625, his stubborn belief in the God-given power of the king set him on a collision course with both Parliament and the heavily taxed City of London. When Charles marched into Parliament to arrest five bolshy MPs (who had fled to the City), Parliament defied him. The country soon slid into civil war.

The City supported Parliament. Defences were built – 30 kilometres of trenches ringed by earthworks – but were never needed. The Civil War rumbled on for several years, but the worst of the fighting ended when Charles I was beheaded outside the Banqueting House in Whitehall in 1649 – wearing two shirts so he wouldn't shiver and seem to be afraid.

From 1653 to 1658, Oliver Cromwell ran the country. A deeply religious man, he shut down theatres and inns and banned make-up, sports, dancing and Christmas decorations. Few Londoners wept when he died, and there were joyful scenes at the restoration parade of Charles II in 1661.

Charles knew how to party and his court was famed for its wild behaviour. But the King did want revenge on his father's killers. The corpses of Cromwell and others were dug up, hung from the gallows at Tyburn, and beheaded. The bodies were then dumped in a pit, while the heads were put on stakes at Westminster until they rotted away.[8]

8. Cromwell's head was on show for 250 years after his death. It now rests in a secret location at Sidney Sussex College, Cambridge.

Pestilence and fire

By 1650, one adult in six in England had lived in London during some part of their life. Overcrowding led to food shortages and disease. The rise in crime meant those who could afford it moved west to Covent Garden and Westminster. From now on, London's rich and poor began to live in different areas.

In 1663, a high tide flooded central London. The River Thames also froze over for several years in the 1660s. At the best of times, the river was full of floating corpses and waste, and at low tide the mudflats stank horribly.

After a run of baking hot summers, in 1665 the Great Plague swept through London. The population hid indoors and London became a ghost town, the streets eerily silent and churches and markets closed. Anyone who could afford to leave scarpered, including the King and court. The highways were chock-a-block with refugees.

No wonder the disease spread so fast – no-one understood what was causing it. Believing that cats and dogs were to blame, the Mayor ordered them killed. At a stroke, he wiped out the natural predators of the real culprits: rats carrying the diseased fleas. To avoid catching the plague, people were told to suck lozenges or smoke tobacco. Others put their faith in lucky charms and magic cures.

In September 1665, over 8,000 people died in a single week. Mercifully, by October the disease had died down, as the unusually cold weather wiped out many of the city's rats. But 100,000 Londoners had already perished. The churchyards were full of rotting flesh, with bodies piled on top of each other.

New burial grounds were created north of the city walls at Moorfields and Stepney, where corpses were gathered and thrown into giant pits. All over the capital, plague pits are linked to local ghosts; some stand empty of buildings even today. If you're the superstitious type, have a wander around Aldgate Tube station. This was built on the site of a plague pit described by writer Daniel Defoe: 1,000 bodies were buried here in only two weeks during 1665.

Just as Londoners breathed a sigh of relief, along came the Great Fire, which effectively razed the old medieval city to the ground. Accidental fires had always been common in the capital – a fire in February 1633 burned for 8 hours and wrecked over 80 houses. But Londoners never learned their lesson and continued to light open fires in houses, shops and workshops. One slip by a tired or drunken neighbour could lead to disaster.

That's exactly what happened one Saturday night in September 1666. A small fire started at Tom Farynor's bakery in Pudding Lane. A strong easterly breeze fanned the flames and blew sparks across the city. Baked by the summer heat, the timber houses that jostled for space inside the city walls soon burst into flames, one street after the next.

The mother of all fires raged for four nights and days, and when it finally died down on the Thursday, the heart of the city was a smouldering ruin. Thankfully, there was plenty of time for people to save not only themselves but many of their belongings, too. Officially, only eight people died in the blaze.

ondon, 1666: the heat is on. Civil servant Sam Pepys escapes by river.

Pepys left a vivid eyewitness account of the Great Fire in his secret diary.

Disaster zone!

- **Plagues.** The Black Death wiped out half of London in 1348. In Tudor times, a mysterious 'sweating sickness' struck at least six times and in 1528 polished off several thousand people in a few hours. Cholera and typhoid were common until the rebuilding of London's sewers in Victorian times.

- **Floods.** In 1579 the Thames rose so high that fish were left stranded in Westminster Hall. As recently as 1953, deadly floods swept much of south-east England, including London.

- **Storms.** In 1090, 600 houses were blown down by a great wind. A hurricane in 1703 blew lead roofing off Westminster Abbey; Queen Anne had to shelter in a cellar at St James's Palace. In 1987 another great storm toppled many of London's plane trees. Bizarrely, sand from the Sahara desert fell on Morden in south London in the same year.

- **Earthquakes.** Yes, really! Quakes were recorded in 1247, 1275, 1382, 1439, 1626 and 1750. The actor Richard Tarleton watched in 1580 as two men sitting on a cannon at Tower Hill were thrown off by a tremor, which also set the City's bells ringing. Don't be too worried – only one Londoner has ever been killed by an earthquake: cobbler Thomas Grey was crushed by falling masonry in Newgate Street (EC1).

- **Tornado.** In December 2006 a tornado ripped through Kensal Green (NW10), injuring six people and damaging over 100 properties.

- **Shipwrecks.** 600 people died when the SS *Princess Alice* sank after a collision with another vessel near Woolwich in 1878. The passengers were either trapped in the sinking craft or thrown into the heavily polluted river – a grim end.

- **Fog and smog.** Charles Dickens called the fog 'London's ivy', as it clung to everything. In the Victorian era half a million coal fires helped to create the phenomenon known as a 'London particular' or 'pea-souper'. Fog caused 700 deaths in 1873, including 19 people who walked into the river, docks or canals. French painter Claude Monet visited London in 1899 and 1901 just to paint fogs. The Great Smog of 1952 was so thick that it crept indoors, forcing cinemas to close and shutting down the ambulance service. Some 12,000 Londoners died in the weeks that followed, most from lung infections.

- **Beer flood.** In 1814 a huge vat containing over 1,470,000 litres of beer collapsed in the Horseshoe Brewery in the district of St Giles (now the site of the Dominion Theatre). The wave of beer destroyed two homes and flooded the cellars of many others, where poor families often lived. Eight people drowned in the flood, while another person died from alcohol poisoning the next day.

Though there were few confirmed deaths, the devastation was second to none. London lost:

- **13,200 houses**
- **80 per cent of the City of London**
- **great buildings including the Guildhall, Royal Exchange and Custom House**
- **St Paul's Cathedral and 87 other churches.**

Some 80,000 Londoners were now homeless. In the winter of 1666 the fields around the capital were strewn with the homeless camping out in tents and shacks. Some went to the suburbs and stayed. Some went to other towns and cities in England, while others went to seek their fortunes in the New World.

Wild rumours spread that the fire was started deliberately by England's enemies – the French, Spanish or Dutch. Mobs roamed the streets, attacking anyone with a dodgy accent.[9] In the end a French watchmaker, Robert Hubert, confessed to the crime. The jury probably knew he was innocent, but sent him to the gallows all the same, while baker Tom Farynor, the guilty party, got off scot-free.

9. One Frenchman was almost torn limb from limb because the mob thought he was carrying firebombs. They were, in fact, tennis balls.

A new start?

The Great Fire provided a once-in-a-lifetime opportunity to give London a logical street system. But any attempt to create a new grid would have led to endless squabbles between landlords and tenants, so the city was rebuilt on the old pattern. A visionary character did came to the rescue, however: Sir Christopher Wren's new St Paul's Cathedral and his 51 other churches defined the London skyline for 300 years and filled the streets with the sound of their bells.[10] Many splendid new theatres were also built, including the Theatre Royal, Drury Lane – which says a lot about London under Charles II!

The Fire Court set up to solve disputes between landlords and tenants acted quickly, and by 1671 some 9,000 houses were rebuilt, mostly in brick instead of wood. Incredibly, the fire didn't slow London down much, though many wealthy merchants were ruined.

10. Many legends surround the rebuilding of London. St Paul's is said to be honeycombed with secret passages. A mummified cat was found in Wren's church of St Michael Paternoster in 1949. Some believe it was sacrificed as part of an ancient rite to bring good luck to the building.

By now, the West End was the place to be. Around this time, Charles moved to St James's Palace and the surrounding area was taken over by rich folk, who moved even further west to be close to the King. Leicester (1671) and Grosvenor (1685) Squares were named after the landlords who built them. They had their own gatekeepers, who keep out flocks of sheep, unwanted tradesmen, and the common mob.

When Charles II died in 1685, his brother James II tried to give Catholics the same rights and freedoms as Protestants. He soon got on the wrong side of Parliament and the London mob. Just three years later, James was given his marching orders and replaced by the Dutch Prince of Orange, who became King William III in 1688.

By 1700 London was the largest city in Europe and one of the most cosmopolitan. In 1685 Protestant refugees arrived in large numbers from France, joining the many Irish, Dutch Jewish and Italian workers already in the city. London also became a centre for science and medicine. Though the Monument

(EC3) was erected as a memorial to the Great Fire of 1666, it also had an underground laboratory and an astronomical observatory on the roof. Scientists such as Robert Hooke (1635–1703), Sir Isaac Newton (1642–1727) and Robert Boyle (1627–1691) came up with the big ideas, but they also relied on London's finest craftworkers for the accurate clocks, telescopes and microscopes they used in their experiments.

If this all sounds thoroughly modern, remember that London was still perhaps the noisiest and most chaotic place in the world, a city filled with horses, cattle, sheep and pigs, driven in great herds through the streets to the slaughterhouses at Smithfield.

Curious customs & traditions

- **Fairs and Festivals.** The 18th-century Horn Fair probably had Celtic origins. Thousands of visitors blew horns as they paraded from Bermondsey (SE1) to Charlton (SE7).

- **Mayfair** (W1). One of London's smartest districts is named after a particularly rowdy Hyde Park festival dating from the late 17th century, awash with pickpockets, gamblers, folk musicians and other ne'er-do-wells.

- **Jack-in-the-Green.** In the 18th and early 19th centuries, sweeps and other tradesmen celebrated May Day by dancing in the streets and playing tricks on each other, led by a giant covered from head to toe in leaves.

- **Rough music** was a way of mocking miscreants such as wife-beaters or women who hen-pecked their husbands. The 'music' was provided by crashing pots and pans, dustbin lids, drums, horns and a good deal of screaming and shouting. The victim might be paraded on a donkey, back to front.

- **Beating the bounds.** This ancient custom marked the bounds of a parish. It is still observed every three years at the Tower of London. On Ascension Day (40 days after Easter) the Chief Yeoman Warder leads a procession around the parish boundaries. At each marker, he cries 'Cursed be he who removeth his neighbour's landmark. Whack it, boys, whack it!" – encouraging a group of local schoolchildren to hit the mark with their willow wands.

- **Raising the dead.** During the 1970s, children could still be seen placing a coin on one of the tombstones in the graveyard at St Mary's, Walthamstow. It was said that if you put sixpence on the grave and danced around it seven times, you could conjure up a ghost!

- **Mock mayors** were once common across England, and the hamlet of Garrett (north of Tooting) was famous for its elections in the 18th century. The idea was to make fun of local officials. Candidates often had ridiculous names such as Lord Twankum or Sir Buggy Bates. After promising the earth, they handed out mock punishments to onlookers. Drunken riots often followed.

- **Grottoes.** Until the 1930s, London children built grottoes in the streets during July and August, hoping to cadge a few pennies from passers-by. Oyster shells, glass, beads and flowers were used to build beehive-shaped towers over a metre high.

- **Traditional games.** In 'ugly bear', one player crawled across the ground getting whacked by the others until he grabbed another player. In 'horny winkles', one team made a bridge of backs while another group leapt on them until the bridge collapsed.

For most, life in Victorian London was no picnic.

*He's a pure-finder; see page 116

CHAPTER THREE

IN FULL SWING

Georgian and Victorian London

During the 18th century, London grew at a terrifying rate, swelling to a million inhabitants by 1800. It spread outwards too, and the old medieval city and Southwark were now ringed by new suburbs. Those who could afford it moved north and west, while those who couldn't headed south and east – divisions that haven't changed much over the years.

New laws helped wealthy landowners become property developers and the elegant squares of the West End multiplied, many taking the names of the men who built them: Curzon, Berkeley, Portman. Fine houses were also built on the roads out of London, in Kensington, Chelsea and Knightsbridge. The medieval bridge was cleared of buildings to ease the flow of traffic, and other crossings were built at Westminster in 1750 and Blackfriars in 1769, opening the way to new suburbs south of the river such as Walworth and Camberwell.

Building and banking went hand in hand. Money was no longer about chests chock-full of gold. William III's chancellor Charles Montagu had created the first state lottery in the 1690s, and ever since, England has been run on credit. The Bank of England was created by Parliament in 1694 to pay for the war against France,[1] and by the 1720s there were 13 banks in London. Between them, they financed the armed forces, wars, city planning and major building projects. The king could do little or nothing without them.[2]

1. The Bank moved to its current address in Threadneedle St in 1734.
2. The bankers, however, weren't working for the government – they were wheeler-dealers looking after their own interests. Sound familiar?

Where to, guv?

Over the centuries, London trades have tended to congregate in certain areas:

- **Doctors and surgeons** in Harley Street
- **Booksellers** in St Paul's Churchyard
- **Tailors** in Savile Row
- **Bird-sellers** in Seven Dials
- **Newspapers** in Fleet Street
- **Jewellers** in Hatton Garden
- **Wheelwrights** in Deptford
- **Saddlers** at Charing Cross
- **Furniture dealers** on Tottenham Court Road
- **Film-makers** in Wardour Street
- **Hat-makers** in Bermondsey

You could buy anything and everything in London. Around 75 per cent of England's trade at this time passed through the capital. It was also the country's manufacturing centre. London was a centre of beer-making[3] and gin distilling as well as the pottery, clockmaking, silk, coachbuilding and furniture industries (the work of cabinetmaker Thomas Chippendale (1718–1779) was famed throughout England.)

3. London's water was usually too filthy to drink, so both grown-ups and children often drank weak beer ('small beer') for breakfast as well as dinner.

Some of London's new-found wealth came at a terrible price – the profitable sugar trade with the West Indies brought misery to many thousands: nearly 750,000 million African slaves were carried in ships sailing from London between 1698 and 1809.[4]

The new flow of money in the capital led to wild speculation. When shares in the South Sea Company soared in 1720, thousands of investors dived in hoping to make a quick buck. The bubble burst and many were ruined. London was badly shaken by the crisis.

Another crisis had loomed 13 years earlier as neither William III nor his sister-in-law Anne, who succeeded him in 1701, had any heirs. In 1707 the English crown passed to George of Hanover, the great-grandson of James I. His reign saw the rise of Robert Walpole, leader of the Whig party and effectively Britain's first prime minister.[5]

4. The slave trade was finally banned in 1806 and slavery itself was abolished in Britain in 1833. By then London already had a distinct black and Asian community, made up of former seamen, servants and slaves. One of the best-known was Ignatius Sancho, a writer and composer who also opened a trendy grocery store in Westminster in 1774.
5. Walpole was given 10 Downing St – he declined the gift, so it became the official residence of every Prime Minister since.

Coffee and chat

Meanwhile, three new drinks changed the habits of a nation. Coffee was introduced in 1650, chocolate in 1657 and tea in 1660. The first coffee house in England was opened in St Michael's Alley, Cornhill in 1652. It was run by Pasqua Rosee, the former servant of a trader in Turkish goods. The drink caught on fast – and within 50 years there were around 2,000 such houses in London.

Some say that newspapers began in the coffee houses, as they were centres of gossip, some of which was written down and circulated. Whether you believe this or not, the newpaper industry flourished on Fleet Street,[6] while Grub Street[7] became notorious for its impoverished hacks churning out rabble-rousing books and pamphlets.

6. In March 1702, London's first daily newspaper, the Daily Courant, was published in Fleet Street from an office above the White Hart Inn – 75 years before the first daily in Paris. By end of the 18th century there were 268 newspapers, journals and periodicals, most published in and around Fleet Street.
7. Now Milton Street (EC2), behind the Barbican complex.

Coffee houses

There was a coffee house for every profession:

- Edward Lloyd's coffee house became a centre for insuring ships and cargoes, the origins of the famous Lloyd's insurance market (still going strong today) which in 1774 moved into the Royal Exchange.

- Will's coffee house was the haunt of politicians and journalists, including Jonathan Swift, the author of *Gulliver's Travels* (1726).

- Garraway's was a magnet for doctors, surgeons and apothecaries (drug-makers).

- Merchants who traded in the West Indies met at the Jerusalem in Cornhill.

- Old Slaughter's Coffee House was popular with artists.

What do you think of Swift's new book?

I can't see it catching on, myself.

Most 18th-century Londoners lived in small rooms and overcrowded houses. They had their fun in taverns, drinking clubs,[8] theatres, coffee houses and pleasure gardens, the best known of these being New Spring Gardens in Vauxhall, Ranelagh Gardens in Chelsea, and Islington Spa. Open to all (at a price), these trendy gardens were the place for ladies and gentleman to flirt, in a way that was simply out of the question in the drawing room.

London's parks have often been called the 'lungs of London'. The large open spaces provided a venue for horse riding, military parades, hunting and 'pistols at dawn'. But footpads and highwaymen lurked in the shadows at night, and even King George II had his 'purse, watch and buckles' stolen from him while taking a turn through Kensington Gardens (W8). Later, the Victorians came up with the idea of planting flowers in parks, though it is said that no flowers grow in Green Park as it was once the burial ground for a local leper's hospital.

8. Drinking clubs were places for singing, smoking and toasting beautiful women. Though some were just an excuse for rowdy behaviour, such as the Farting Club and the Mock Heroes Club, others were a place for serious political debate, such as the Kit-Cat Club.

Great minds were drawn to the capital. In 1755 Dr Samuel Johnson produced the first English dictionary. George Frederick Handel wrote his *Water Music* (1717) and *Messiah* (1741) while living in the capital, which also attracted famous painters such as Thomas Gainsborough (1727–1788) and Sir Joshua Reynolds (1723–1792). Grand theatres such as the Haymarket and Covent Garden flourished, though Cockney theatre-goers often liked to shout insults down from the gallery and pelt performers with fruit. Riots were common, and rival groups even paid boxers to help them slug it out.

Plenty of lowbrow entertainments were available too. Bear-baiting was lawful until 1835. Cockfighting took place quite openly on the streets of London until the 1840s, while mud-wrestling in Belsize Park was so popular in the 1730s that it had to be closed down. Shame…

Bear-baiting

The flip side of success

Though this all seems very jolly, London was turning into two cities. While the wealthy lived in fine houses and chatted in fashionable coffee houses in the West End, on the other side of town the poor shivered in miserable slums and drank themselves to death.

Not for the first time, the sheer size of London led to poverty and misery on a huge scale. London was notorious for its many prostitutes, 'bawdy houses' (brothels) and street children. Though poorhouses had been created to help the very poor, the old and the sick, they were replaced in the 1720s by workhouses. These were little more than prisons where inmates worked 12-hour shifts in filthy conditions.

Poor districts such as Holborn and St Giles were rabbit warrens of dark, dirty alleyways where falling tiles and rickety walls were a constant threat to life and limb. As the better-off moved to the West End, in came the street sellers, labourers and criminals. In poor areas, gin was easier to find than clean water. It was dirt-cheap (twopence bought enough gin to get you dead drunk) – and addictive. Gin-drinking was soon London's biggest social problem.[9] Despite new laws to control the sale of the demon drink, the death toll continued to mount.

Unruly mobs were a constant menace, and they frequently took their anger out on foreigners. In 1762, Scottish writer James Boswell watched in horror when two Scottish army officers were pelted with apples as they went to watch a play at Covent Garden.

The mobs were often made up of disgruntled workers such as silk weavers or hatmakers, who had no other way of protesting at low wages or a fall in trade. But not all gangs on the street were poor. The 'Mohocks', who took their name from the Mohawk tribe in North America, came from wealthy families and attacked people just for fun. Prowling the streets with lighted torches, they formed a circle around their victims and prodded and slashed at them with their swords.

9. By 1723 London was drinking the equivalent of a pint of gin each week for every man, woman and child.

In 1780, Parliament proposed lifting a law that prevented Catholics from buying or inheriting property. Around 60,000 Londoners took to the streets in protest, led by Lord George Gordon, leader of the Protestant Association. They marched across the Thames to hand a 'No Popery' petition to Parliament, but soon all hell broke loose.

The mob began looting and burning Catholic churches and homes and attacking Irish labourers. Then groups of sailors and others attacked Newgate prison, freeing the inmates. For several nights, London's poor showed just what they thought of the rich. They attacked law courts and the homes of judges and even attempted to break into the Bank of England. After six days of mayhem, 10,000 soldiers put a stop to the riots and 25 ringleaders were hanged. Over 250 people died during the Gordon Riots, including one group that drank themselves to death after breaking into a gin factory in Holborn.

Riots, rebellions and sieges

The Gordon Riots of 1780 were just part of a
long tradition of violence and rebellion:

- **The Peasants' Revolt, 1381.** (See page 60.)

- **Evil May Day, 1517.** A mob of around 1,000
  apprentices rioted in protest against foreign
  merchants and craftworkers. Though no-one
  was killed, they attacked and burnt many
  houses and workshops belonging to Flemish,
  French and Italian traders. Troops arrested
  over 300 rioters; 13 were convicted of
  treason and hung, drawn and quartered.

- **Bawdy House Riots 1668.** Apprentices
  attacked brothels throughout London, fed up
  with the wicked ways of Charles II's courtiers.

- **Spitalfields Riots, 1769.** Riots among the
  Spitalfields weavers were common in the 18th
  century, in protest against low wages. When
  soldiers tried to arrest a group of weavers in
  September 1769, they fought back. Two men
  were shot and another two hanged.

- **Old Price Riots, 1809.** When Covent Garden
  theatre was rebuilt after a fire, the prices
  were put up. Audiences brought in whistles,
  drums and even farmyard animals to disrupt
  performances. This continued until the old
  prices were brought back and the manager
  apologised on stage.

- **Black Monday, 1886.** A protest over unemployment led to a riot in Pall Mall. The police looked on as rioters smashed windows and attacked onlookers, and the head of the Metropolitan Police was sacked soon after.

- **Sidney Sreet Siege, 1911.** When the police learned that an anarchist gang wanted for armed robbery was holed up inside no. 100 Sidney St, Home Secretary Winston Churchill called in the army. During the shoot-out, the building caught fire. When the police moved in they found the bodies of two men, one shot by a police marksman and the other killed by the smoke.

- **Battle of Bow Street, 1919.** This riot kicked off after policemen tried to stop Australian and US soldiers and sailors playing dice on the Strand. When a rumour went round that one man had died in police custody, an angry crowd began attacking the Bow Street police station. It took repeated charges by police on foot and on horseback to quell the mob.

- **Poll Tax Riots, 1990.** When Prime Minister Margaret Thatcher tried to reintroduce a flat-rate tax, 600 years after the poll tax that sparked the Peasants' Revolt, a demonstration in Trafalgar Square erupted into the worst riots of the century. Cars were overturned and set on fire and many shop windows were smashed. There were 340 arrests and 100 were injured, including 45 police officers.

Given that London was dogged by crime in those days, you might be shocked to learn that just 300 unarmed, part-time constables patrolled its streets. You'd be less surprised to know that some parts of the capital were no-go areas ruled by gangs. Until the 18th century, London's streets were guarded by its citizens, who took turns to watch from the city walls and patrol the streets on foot. These watchmen, or 'Charleys', were figures of fun and were frequently attacked in public. In the 1750s Henry Fielding set up the Bow Street Runners, nicknamed 'Raw Lobsters' due to their red vests. But it soon became clear that the Runners were in cahoots with the villains.

Prisons and harsh punishments were the main weapons in the fight against crime. For lesser crimes, you could be punished by being:

- dragged through the streets
- fined
- whipped
- put in the pillory, where passers-by could hurl abuse and rotten food at you
- branded with a hot iron
- shipped to the Americas or (later) Australia.

Bobbies, coppers or rozzers?

- In 1829, Sir Robert Peel set up the Metropolitan Police Force in Great Scotland Yard with a force of 3,000 men. They were called 'bobbies' or 'peelers' after their founder.

> We didn't wear those silly hats in my day.

- The terms 'coppers' and 'Old Bill' have their origins in the bands of copper and the royal symbol for William IV found on the first truncheons.

Bow Street Runner

> If you find yourself on the wrong side of the law, 'Sir' often works best!

- 'Rozzers' comes from the East End slang for 'roasting'.

- 'The fuzz' may come from the sound of the first police radios. It was originally a US word for the police from the 1930s.

London rogues

- **Moll Cutpurse.** A former actress, Mary Frith was a pickpocket who later turned to highway robbery dressed as a man. After a short prison sentence, she turned to selling stolen goods and died at her home in Fleet Street in 1674.

- Royalist **Miles Sindercombe** tried to assassinate Oliver Cromwell more than once, even planting a bomb at Whitehall Palace, but failed miserably. Sindercombe's nose was cut off in a fight with Cromwell's spymaster John Thurloe, but he escaped the traitor's sentence of being hung, drawn and quartered by taking poison in 1657.

- Irish-born **Colonel Blood** tried to steal the Crown Jewels from the Tower of London in 1671. After knocking out one of the guards, Blood and two accomplices stuffed the jewels into their clothes but were chased and caught. Remarkably, Blood was pardoned by Charles II, who perhaps had a sneaking admiration for the bold scoundrel.

- **Jack Collett.** The 17th-century highwayman was famous for robbing travellers while dressed as a bishop. Though he lost his outfit in a game of dice, soon afterwards he stopped the Bishop of Winchester on the road from London to Farnham, who reluctantly handed his money – and his robes – over to Collett.

The highwayman's luck ran out in 1691 when he was caught and hanged after robbing Great St Bartholomew's in London.

- **Claude Duval.** The dashing French highwayman had a reputation for robbing stagecoaches without resorting to violence. In one story he relieved a gentleman of £100 after dancing with his wife by the roadside. When he was eventually arrested at the Hole-in-the-Wall pub in Chandos Street in 1670, several ladies at court pleaded for him, but he hanged all the same. His memorial in St Paul's, Covent Garden reads: 'Here lies Duval: reader, if male thou art, Look to thy purse; if female, to thy heart.'

- **Sixteen-String Jack.** Highwayman John Rann got his nickname from the coloured strings on the knees of his silk breeches. No master criminal, he was arrested several times for robbery but let off due to lack of evidence. His luck ran out in 1774, but, elegant to the last, he went to the gallows at Tyburn dressed in a pea-green suit, aged just 24.

- **Jonathan Wild.** This 18th-century gangster ran a vast criminal empire based on stealing property then selling it back to the owners. Any of his men who stepped out of line were handed over to the police, giving Wild the image of a law-abiding 'Thief-Taker General'. The truth caught up with him in 1725, when he was arrested and hanged for trying to spring one of his men out of Newgate prison.

Though hundreds of crimes were punished by hanging, most of those who went to the gallows were convicted of theft.

While Parliament paid for its wars and grand buildings by borrowing huge sums of money, even those with small debts were flung in prison. Some prisoners were allowed to work to pay off their debts; others stayed for decades or even died in their cells.[10] Today's criminal court at Old Bailey stands on the site of Newgate, a prison known as the 'tomb for the living' as so many of its inmates died from diseases such as cholera and typhoid.

All prisons at this time were privately run for profit, so how you were treated depended on how rich you were. Blackmail and torture were rife, and the conditions in most prisons were appalling. Most were horribly overcrowded. From 1776, convicts were imprisoned in the hulks of old warships moored on the Thames off Woolwich.

10. In 1729, 300 people starved to death over a three-month period in just one London prison, Marshalsea. (Charles Dickens's father was sent there in 1824 for a debt of £40 and 10 shillings.)

The height of fashion

Victory over France in 1815 led to a new swagger in England, and a flurry of new churches, monuments and statues.[11]

The Prince Regent, the future George IV, was a big property developer who was determined to drag London into the 19th century. Architect John Nash (1752–1835) planned a new 'spine' for London, running south from the new Regent's Park to St James's Park. Other developments included Piccadilly Circus, Trafalgar Square and landmark buildings such as the British Musueum and the National Gallery. London now saw itself as the capital of Europe.

The West End became a mecca for shoppers. Window-shopping was the in thing once the first plate-glass windows appeared. Other novelties included arcades and bazaars – covered shopping areas that could be enjoyed on rainy days. Shops opened on Sundays, the day after most people got paid.

11. *London remembers its heroes and battles in street and place names: Trafalgar Square, Waterloo Station, and over 25 Wellington Roads.*

Nelson's Column

- If you believe some people, Nelson's column is exactly the right height for the Admiral to see the sea (not true). However, the statue does face south, where Nelson's Flagship HMS *Victory* is docked. A laser survey in 2006 found that it was around 50 metres tall – 6 metres shorter than previously thought.

- In another tale, it is said that the four giant bronze lions at the bottom of the column face outwards to guard Nelson. They were added to the column in 1868, some 25 years late. The delay by the sculptor Sir Edwin Landseer became a running joke in the newspapers.

- Before Nelson's statue was hauled into place, the 14 stonemasons on the job enjoyed a party on the platform at the top.

- In 1925 a Scottish confidence trickster, Arthur Furguson, 'sold' the landmark to an American tourist for £6,000.

- If Hitler's plan to invade Britain, Operation Sealion, had been successful, the SS planned to ship Nelson's Column to Berlin.

- In May 2003 stuntman Gary Connery parachuted from the top of the column to protest at the Chinese occupation of Tibet.

I see no ships!
But you'd be surprised
what I *can* see from
up here.

Nelson on his column:
one eye, one arm, and
not as tall as he looks.

Historic shops

- **Burlington Arcade,** Piccadilly. The longest covered shopping street in Britain is also the oldest, opened in 1819. Running, umbrellas and whistling are all forbidden; the rules are enforced by traditional security guards called 'beadles' in top hats and tails.

- **Harrods,** Knightsbridge. The biggest department store in Britain has 90,000 square metres of selling space in over 330 departments. Its motto is *Omnia omnibus ubique* – 'All things for all people, everywhere'.

- **Selfridges,** Oxford St. This department store was the latest thing in shopping when it opened in 1909. The American owner, Gordon Selfridge, installed a personal lift in the store so friends could come and go in private. He came up with the slogan 'The customer is always right.'

- **Hamley's,** Regent St. Founded by William Hamley in 1760, who created a 'Noah's Ark' stuffed with toys, the store was already a London landmark when Queen Victoria came to the throne in 1837. It moved to its current building in 1881.

- **Liberty's,** off Regent St, opened in 1875 selling ornaments, fabrics and fine art from Japan and the Far East. The splendid Tudor-style building that houses the shop today was built in the 1920s. To create the feeling that shoppers were walking around their own home, many of the rooms were small and had their own fireplaces.

- **Fortnum & Mason,** Piccadilly. When William Fortnum and Hugh Mason set up shop in 1707, Fortnum was a footman in the household of Queen Anne. The royal family insisted on having new candles every night, and using the left-over wax the two men went into business selling candles. The store has often led the way in introducing new tastes: in 1851 it created the Scotch egg and in 1886 it was the first store in the world to stock the baked beans invented by Mr H. J. Heinz.

- **Twining & Co.,** the Strand. At a time when coffee shops were all the rage, Thomas Twining opened the first known tea room in Britain in 1706. In 1834 the then prime minister, Charles Grey, 2nd Earl Grey, asked the firm to match a sample of tea he had been given by a Chinese official whose son had been saved from drowning by one of the Earl's men. The result was Earl Grey tea, known for its trademark citrus taste.

Victorian London

When Queen Victoria came to the throne in 1837 at the age of 18, it marked the beginning of an era in which London life accelerated at a dizzying pace. If the city was already a centre for global trade and industry, this new industrial revolution sent it into overdrive. Small cottage industries were overtaken by great factories belching smoke, and London's brewing, leatherworking, engineering and shipbuilding industries all flourished.

New laws in 1762 had not only paved the streets in stone but led to iron water pipes, state-of-the art gas lighting, and even a tunnel under the Thames. 19th-century London was further transformed by the coming of the railways, though this didn't seem quite so wonderful if you happened to live in one of the neighbourhoods torn down to make way for the new tracks, stations and shunting yards.

The first railway line in the capital, built in 1836, ran from London Bridge to Greenwich. This was soon followed by the opening of the great railway stations, which by the 1850s linked London via a network of tracks to the Midlands, the west, the north, Scotland and Wales.[12] Metropolitan railways linked the city centre to the burgeoning suburbs, and the middle class could now commute into town, leaving the inner city to the poor.

A new docks complex in the East End dealt with the influx in trade from the colonies, though some London trades suffered due to cheap imports and rivalry with factories in the north and Midlands. London was the hub of the largest and richest empire on the planet, which at its height covered a quarter of the world's land surface and ruled 500 million people. It was also the centre of world banking, and purpose-built offices sprang up.

By now the city had its first professional police force, established in 1829. At first Londoners had little respect for the 'boys in blue', but attitudes changed after the Coldbath Fields riot in 1833 when the police broke up a mob without any serious injuries to the crowd – though one constable was stabbed to death.

12. The new stations included Euston (1837), Paddington (1838), Fenchurch Street (1841), Waterloo (1848), King's Cross (1850) and St Pancras (1863).

Though every Londoner knows that Scotland Yard is the headquarters of the Metropolitan Police, few stop to wonder how it got its name. Until the Act of Union in 1707, Scotland was a separate country with its own rules and laws. (There are still many differences today.) Like any other country, it had an embassy in London – now Great Scotland Yard. Curiously, like any other embassy, the street is in theory still part of Scottish territory.

Unlike Paris, London was never really a hotbed of radicals and revolution – perhaps because anyone who complained too loudly got shipped off to the colonies in Australia and Canada. Nonetheless, by the 1830s its citizens were increasingly unhappy that only the rich and the wealthier middle classes had the vote.[13] In 1848, the Chartist movement hoped that 100,000 people would march on Parliament to present a petition (the Charter giving the movement its name), demanding a vote for every man in Britain. Though only 20,000 turned up, the government wasn't taking any chances and over 7,000 troops were drafted in.

13. Even after the 1832 Reform Act, just 7 per cent of men could vote – and no women.

The workshop of the world

When Queen Victoria opened the Great Exhibition in the Crystal Palace on 1 May 1851, Britain had a chance to show the rest of the world just how brilliant it was:

- The huge glass, iron and timber 'palace' was 560 m long and 30 m high.
- Designed by Joseph Paxton, it was built in just 7 months, using 300,000 panes of glass and 48 km of guttering.
- The exhibition was home to 100,000 exhibits from every corner of the British Empire, displayed on 16 km of stands.
- It brought thousands of tourists to London and 300,000 people turned up at Hyde Park to watch the opening ceremony.
- It made so much money that London went on to build the complex of museums in South Kensington that now includes the Victoria and Albert, Natural History and Science Museums, as well as the Royal Albert Hall.

London itself was home to railways, steamships and other wonders of the modern world such as the penny post and the electric telegraph. By 1875, a network of over 380 trams (coaches on rails pulled by two horses) carried around 49 million Londoners every year on 100 km of track. Famous landmarks built at this time include the Houses of Parliament (1852), its clock tower 'Big Ben' (1859) and Tower Bridge (1894). Yet despite the Victorians' unshakable belief in progress, below the arches of their grand railway stations, poor children starved to death.

In Victorian London,
new technology and slum housing
lived side by side.

By 1871 there were over 3 million people living in the capital, and this doubled to 6 million by 1900. Many of the newcomers were refugees from the Great Famine in Ireland (1845–1849); in late Victorian times Irish immigrants made up about 20 per cent of London's population.

Overcrowding led to horrific slums, endless traffic jams and the constant threat of cholera, which killed tens of thousands of Londoners in the 19th century.[14] Death was ever-present in Victorian times: 3 out of every 20 babies died before their first birthday, and adults were lucky to live beyond 40.

Henry Mayhew's survey of London's poor, carried out in the 1850s, is crammed with beggars, barefooted street sellers and 'sweathouse' labourers working long hours for little pay. Charles Dickens, a champion of the poor, shocked his readers with unforgettable images of ragged street urchins, brutal workhouses and slave-driving factory owners.

14. In just one year – 1849 – 14,000 Londoners died from cholera.

Someone's got to do it...

There have always been plenty of interesting jobs in the city to pick from:

- **Ravenmaster.** This official still has the vital job of ensuring that the ravens don't leave the Tower of London – easy enough, you'd think, given that the birds' wings are clipped.

- **City Garbler.** An official with the power to enter any shop and examine the drugs and spices on sale by 'garbling' (sifting) them.

- **Watermen.** Until Victorian times, the Thames was London's main highway. Watermen ferried people and goods in small rowing boats known as *wherries*.

- **Dung removal.** In Tudor times, gong-farmers removed the dung or 'gong' from private toilets (a.k.a. 'privies', 'cludgies' or 'thunderboxes') for use as manure. In the 19th century, nightsoil men cleaned the city's cesspits, while 'pure-finders' roamed the streets scooping up dog poop, or 'pure', which was used for tanning leather.

- **Costermongers.** These street hawkers got their name from the 'costard' apple grown in orchards around the capital. They attracted customers with their singsong cry and cheeky banter. In Victorian times, every marketplace had its own 'Coster King'.

- **Searchers of the dead** were paid to spot plague victims and mark their houses with a red cross. This unpopular job was was mostly done by poor, older women. During the Great Plague of 1665, their wages plummeted as the city couldn't afford to pay for the hundreds of people dying every day.

- **Herb-strewer.** In the 17th and 18th centuries a full-time servant was paid to leave sweet-smelling herbs and flowers in the rooms of the royal home, to block out the stench from London's open sewers.

- **Sewer workers.** Whole families worked as 'toshers' and 'grubbers', scouring the sewers for anything of value. The flushermen who cleared blockages in the sewer system wore long blue overcoats and thigh-length waders, unlike the barefooted mudlarks, small children who also made a living by poking around in sewers and the mudbanks on the Thames.

- **Rat-catchers** were paid by the city to prevent the spread of disease. Queen Victoria's rat-catcher, Jack Black, was known for his scarlet coat and wide leather belt decorated with cast-iron rats.

- **Fluffers.** A band of night-time workers still enter the Underground tunnels every night to remove all the human hair and bits of dead skin that build up during the day. Though machines are used, some of the debris is still removed by hand using brushes and brooms.

Wives going cheap

Even in the 19th century, wife-selling was a way of getting a 'quickie' divorce in London. Most auctions took place at the local market, and the husband would simply pay the fee needed to register as a seller. Traditionally the wife wore a collar and lead, to reinforce the resemblance to a livestock sale. Some wives were even sold by weight, like cattle. Though this sounds dreadful, in many cases the wife already knew who was going to buy her, and the auction simply allowed her to marry her lover.

By now the city's foul-smelling cesspits were overflowing and fouling the public drinking water. The old-fashioned system of local parishes struggled to cope with the rapid growth in population, so in 1855 the Metropolitan Board of Works was set up to tackle the source of the city's diseases – the waterworks. Raw sewage was being pumped straight into the River Thames – the origin of the 'Great Stink' of 1858. The pong from the river forced Parliament to protect itself with chlorine-soaked sheets draped over the windows. The creation of the London sewers, masterminded by Sir Joseph Bazalgette, is one of the triumphs of Victorian engineering.[15]

Other improvements included the appearance of specialist hospitals such as Great Ormond Street (for children), and a modern fire-fighting service organised by London hero James Braidwood, who died fighting a giant blaze in Tooley St (SE1).

The streets of Victorian London were jammed with horsedrawn vehicles such as omnibuses, which competed with the old hackney carriages. From the 1840s, steamboats added to the traffic along the Thames.

The poor had few pleasures. One was smoking – Sir Walter Raleigh possibly first smoked tobacco in Islington in the late 16th century. By the 17th century men, women and children smoked all over London. At first clay pipes were used; cigarettes arrived after the Crimean War (1854–1856), and the first cigarette factory opened in Walworth in 1857.

15. Around 1,700 km of new sewers were built, while existing drains were lined with cement.

The other distraction from the horrors of the slums was drink. There was a boom in public houses in the 1890s and 1900s (the Victorians were the first call their watering holes 'pubs'). Many pub names reflect historic or local events; others gave their names to nearby Tube stations – Elephant & Castle, Royal Oak, Swiss Cottage and the Angel, Islington.

Working-class Londoners also flocked to the music halls that developed from small singing rooms at the back of pubs. Stars such as Dan Leno and Marie Lloyd were household names. The large arena at Earl's Court (W12) hosted shows from the United States, including Buffalo Bill Cody's Wild West Show and Barnum & Bailey's circus, which staged spectacular chariot races and gladiator fights.

In the 1830s, gentleman's clubs sprang up along Pall Mall, while in the second half of the 19th century the Café Royal became the late-night hang-out of intellectuals such as writer Oscar Wilde and painter J. M. Whistler. Hampstead, Holland Park and St John's Wood were all home to famous artists' communities.

Bizarre pub names

- **I Am the Only Running Footman.** Footmen were paid to run ahead of their master's carriage to clear the way and pay the tolls.

- **Lamb & Flag.** Probably the oldest pub in Covent Garden, this was once named the Bucket of Blood as it was a venue for illegal bare-knuckle fights.

- **Queen's Larder.** While King George III was being treated for madness in Queen's Square, his wife Queen Charlotte rented a place nearby to store food.

- **Blue Posts.** Several pubs in the West End have this name: they were a pick-up point for sedan chairs (carried on two poles by bearers), marked by two poles painted blue.

- **Magpie & Stump.** Until public hangings were abolished in 1868, this pub used to charge extra for drinks taken upstairs, where customers got a great view of the hangings outside Newgate prison.

- **Widow's Son.** Every Good Friday, a sailor hangs a hot-cross bun over the bar. The legend goes that an elderly widow baked a bun each year in the hope that her son, a sailor, would return home. As the years passed, the buns multiplied.

By the end of the century London was grander then ever, and terribly pleased with itself. There were long celebrations to mark Queen Victoria's Golden and Diamond Jubilees. The city spread slowly outwards. In 1861 only 400,000 Londoners lived in the suburbs, but by 1911 the figure was 2.7 million, partly due to the city's newly electrified transport system.

Building the Underground was a mammoth task. The first Tube line, the Metropolitan, opened in 1863, and within 12 years there were 100 km of track, allowing Londoners to travel cheaply and quickly around town.

The new middle-class Londoners who lived in the suburbs worked less but shopped more. Department stores were modelled on those in fashionable Paris, which along with New York was starting to rival London as the world's greatest city. In the centre of town, giant flagships such as Harrods offered the world – at a price – while by 1900 Jesse Boot's chain of chemists' and John Sainsbury's grocery stores were an increasingly common sight on suburban high streets.

During the 18th century, Londoners had eaten out in chop-houses, dining in groups around large tables, but from the 1860s people increasingly ate in restaurants and dining rooms. Women were allowed to join the men for the evening meal for the first time in centuries, and dinner-dances were all the rage.

While those at the bottom of the heap still lived in great poverty, the growth of the trade unions gave them power and confidence, seen in the match girls' strike of 1888[16] and the dockers' strike a year later. Cheap labour poured into London – farm workers from the provinces, Irish immigrants, and Jewish refugees fleeing from persecution in Russia and eastern Europe.

I should skip the next few pages if you're of a nervous disposition.

16. Women at the Bryant and May factory in Bow went on strike after one of their fellow workers was sacked. But the real cause of the strike was poor working conditions, including 14-hour work days, low pay, and the hazards of handling the phosphorus used to make matches.

Jack the Ripper

In four short months in 1888, a serial killer butchered at least five women in Whitechapel by cutting their throats and removing their innards. This remains one of the most famous unsolved cases in the world, and there are dozens of theories about who the killer really was:

- At the time the police suspected several men, including Montague John Druitt, a schoolteacher who killed himself shortly after the murders, and George Chapman, who poisoned three of his wives.

- Other suspects at the time included Neill Cream, a doctor, as the wounds looked as though they had been made by someone who knew how to use a scalpel. Sir Arthur Conan Doyle, creator of the famous detective Sherlock Holmes, put forward the theory that the crimes had been carried out by a man dressed as a woman – 'Jill the Ripper'.

- Several authors have pointed the finger at Prince Albert Victor, nicknamed 'Eddy', Queen Victoria's grandson. One theory suggests James Kelly, who had murdered his wife in 1883 by stabbing her in the neck. An American researcher argued that the Ripper was in fact Lewis Carroll (real name Charles Lutwidge Dodgson), author of *Alice in Wonderland* (1865)!

- Several hoax letters were sent to the police, including a postcard in October 1888 that read: 'You'll hear about Saucy Jacky's work tomorrow. Double event this time. Number one squealed a bit, Couldn't finish straight off. Had not time to get ears for police.' Another parcel contained half a human kidney preserved in wine along with a letter that signed off: 'Catch me when you can.'

- Jack the Ripper became a bogeyman used to frighten naughty children – an evil monster who lurked in the foggy streets.

- Perhaps the only good to come from the case was the fact that it highlighted the terrible living conditions in much of the East End, leading to two important new laws in 1890. Over the next 20 years, many of the worst slums were finally cleared.

Haunted London

- **50 Berkeley Square.** Called the 'most haunted house in London' after two sailors spent the night there. One was found impaled on the railings outside, while the other went mad.

- **Bank of England.** A young bank employee was hanged for forging cheques in 1811. His sister came to the bank every day to ask for him. After she died, her ghost, the 'Bank Nun', was said to haunt the building.

- **Blackfriars Bridge.** In the 1930s a young woman was seen jumping off the bridge seven days in a row, the ghost of a suicide victim.

- **Tower of London.** Famous ghosts include a headless Anne Boleyn, Walter Raleigh, and the Princes in the Tower. Late-night security guards report spooky smells and ghostly chills.

- **Maida Vale.** A hideous pig-faced lady was seen haunting a garden here in 1912, and again a fortnight later.

- **Aldgate.** A shadowy old woman was seen by a railway worker just before he touched a live wire and was blasted by 20,000 volts. Amazingly, he survived.

- **University College London.** The philosopher Jeremy Bentham supposedly paces the corridors, tapping his walking stick.

126

Though the Metropolitan Police cut crime in the capital, during the 1880s there were still parts of London ruled by criminal gangs, such as Hoxton (E8), the 'Rookeries' of Seven Dials (WC2) and the notorious 'Nichol' area of Shoreditch (EC2) where rival gangs fought on the streets. Cheap booklets known as 'penny dreadfuls' scared the living daylights out of Londoners with tall tales about Sweeney Todd, the demon barber of Fleet Street (EC4), and the murderous innkeeper of Farringdon Street (EC1).

Victorian London did try to sort itself out. When she came to the throne, Queen Victoria made the monarchy respectable again after the wild excesses of George IV. When her husband Albert died in 1861, Victoria went into mourning and retired from public life. Her restrained behaviour set the tone of the age – the Victorians were rather a stuffy lot.

The 1870 Education Act led to 500 new schools in just 30 years, though in 1901 some 300,000 children were still working to support their families. But by the end of the century most Londoners could read and write.

Londoners have remained great readers – just look down a crowded train or Tube carriage to see a forest of books and newspapers.

There was plenty of reading to be done – Victorian Londoners included poet Elizabeth Barrett Browning and novelists William Makepeace Thackeray, Arthur Conan Doyle and Anthony Trollope, who is also credited with inventing London's red postboxes. Most of Charles Dickens's works first appeared in affordable monthly instalments.

Victorian science was dominated by Charles Darwin, whose book *On the Origin of Species* (1859) still creates controversy today. Charles Babbage came up with the idea of mechanical thinking machines, the forerunners of modern computers, while surgeon John Snow was one of the first scientists to make the link between cholera and contaminated water.

When Queen Victoria died in 1901, London was still a city of great extremes. Though her capital dominated the world, the Queen still got booed every time she showed her face in the East End!

CHAPTER FOUR

A CHANGING WORLD
Two world wars - and after

dward VII, Queen Victoria's son, was already 60 when he came to the throne in 1901. In contrast to his mother, here was someone who enjoyed life to the full, from illegal card games and betting at the races to smoking cigars or enjoying lavish dinner parties with one of his many lady friends.[1]

---

1. *Edward certainly loved his food: he began the tradition of leaving the bottom button on a suit undone, mainly because of his tubby 48-inch (122-cm) waist. The King also introduced the idea of the 'Sunday lunch' of roast beef, roast potatoes and Yorkshire pudding.*

This popular king, whose friends included grocers as well as nobles, brought a new flavour to London, still the largest city in the world.[2] Several major building projects underlined the city's role as a great imperial capital. Architect Aston Webb designed the long, broad sweep of the Mall, Admiralty Arch[3] and the Queen Victoria memorial.

The Edwardian era saw the building of Waterloo Station, the redevelopment of Kingsway (WC2),[4] and a rash of new monuments, including the Blue Plaque scheme that linked London's buildings with famous people and events. Londoners could also be proud of the new stadium built in double-quick time at White City (W12) for the 1908 Olympics after an eruption of Mount Vesuvius devastated Naples and forced the games to be switched from Italy.

The Great Exhibition of 1851 kick-started the London tourist industry, and by the 1860s

2. London hit the 7 million mark in 1911, while its nearest rival, New York, was home to just under 5 million people.
3. A small bump in the wall of the Arch is said to be Napoleon's nose – if you ride through on horseback you can touch it for good luck!
4. Named after the King, and at that time London's widest street.

the capital had its first big hotels: the Westminster Palace Hotel had 300 bedrooms and the first lifts in London. The 1900s brought a rash of new luxury hotels and department stores: the Ritz Hotel opened in 1906, Harrods completed its flagship store in Knightsbridge in 1905, and Selfridges opened its doors on Oxford Street in 1907. New venues sprang up all over London, especially in the West End, where the London Palladium was the largest of 60 large theatres offering music-hall and variety shows.

The turn of the century was also a time of new technology. In 1904 (a year after the Wright Brothers' first flight in the USA) London's first motor bus appeared, followed by the first electric Underground train in 1906. Better transport was good for the West End, which by the beginning of the First World War was very much the place we know today. People from the suburbs headed into town to enjoy its theatres and cinemas. (Cinemas had appeared in the 1890s and were an instant hit.) Londoners generally had more money in their pockets and shopping and eating out were increasingly popular.

London County Council tried to improve life for all by clearing the worst slums, building public baths and libraries, and installing electric lighting. In 1888, Electric Avenue in Brixton had become the first shopping street to be lit by electricity.

The Suffragette movement that demanded the vote for Britain's women moved its campaign to London in 1903, promising 'Deeds not Words'. Led by Emmeline Pankhurst and her daughters, the Suffragettes held monster rallies in Hyde Park and chained themselves to government buildings. When this didn't work, they went on the rampage in central London, smashing shop windows and attacking famous works of art.

Out with the old

Many old markets were swept away by new developments in the 19th and 20th centuries. The rebuilding of Aldwych and Kingsway in 1900 saw the end of Clare Market, built by the Earl of Clare 250 years earlier. The market was famous for its butchers and for the tradition of serenading newlyweds with marrowbones and cleavers specially chosen to form a complete octave of notes!

N ot everyone
approved of votes
for women.

Young Hot~Bloods

Within the Suffragette movement, a secret group known as the Young Hot-Bloods carried out 'danger duty' – brave acts that would grab the nation's attention. When Emily Wilding Davison died after throwing herself in front of the King's horse at the Epsom Derby in June 1913, she had already:

- started a fire in the General Post Office and set fire to pillar-boxes

- hidden herself three times in the House of Commons, once in a hot-air shaft

- been put in prison nine times

- gone on hunger-strike three times and barricaded herself in a prison cell

- tried to commit suicide by throwing herself down an iron staircase in Holloway prison in protest against forced feeding

- planted a bomb at the house of the Chancellor of the Exchequer, David Lloyd George, badly damaging it.

The 'War to End All Wars'

When the First World War began in August 1914, few realised the impact it would have on the capital. The first Zeppelins[5] dropped their bombs on London a year later, followed by planes later in the war. Though 670 Londoners were killed in these raids, it was nothing compared to the slaughter of millions in the trenches. In fact, the largest explosion in the city occurred by accident, when 50 tonnes of TNT blew up in a munitions factory at Silvertown in West Ham (E13).

5. Rigid-bodied airships named after their creator, the German Count Ferdinand von Zeppelin (1838–1917).

Even so, the city's confidence was rocked by the bombing, along with food shortages caused by U-boat (submarine) attacks on British shipping. With the men at the front lines, London's women did their bit for the war effort as factory or transport workers. Emmeline Pankhurst instructed the Suffragettes to support the government in every way, and at the end of the war, Parliament finally gave women the vote.[6]

The London mob, meanwhile, now had the perfect excuse to attack anyone or anything vaguely German- or foreign-sounding. Even the 400,000 or so Belgian and French refugees who arrived in London during the war were made to feel less than welcome. Surprisingly, it took three years of war for King George V to realise it might be a good idea to change the royal family's name from Saxe-Coburg-Gotha (very German) to Windsor (thoroughly English).

Those who came back from the war were promised 'a land fit for heroes'. The end of the Great War did bring a new mood to the city –

6. Lady Astor became the first female member of Parliament in 1919.

many young people had been made old by the horrors of war, and there was a general feeling that life was short and should be enjoyed.

London in the Jazz Age of the 1920s was typified by the rebuilt West End with its bright lights. A major facelift for Regent Street included a shiny new Underground station at Piccadilly Circus that could cope with 50 million passengers a year. Londoners of all classes headed 'up West' to dance the night away or watch a movie with 2,400 others at the Regal 'super-cinema' at Marble Arch.

The arts in London flourished, most famously the 'Bloomsbury set', a group of intellectuals that included writer Virginia Woolf and economist John Maynard Keynes. In the 1930s, the Fitzrovia Tavern in Charlotte Street (W1) became the favourite watering-hole of writer George Orwell and Welsh poet Dylan Thomas.

From 1920, London's famous red telephone boxes began to appear on the streets, designed by Sir Giles Gilbert Scott.

London in song

Hundreds of songs namecheck London. Here are just a few:

Burlington Bertie from Bow Harry B. Norris
Let's All Go Down the Strand Castling/Murphy
A Foggy Day in London Town George Gershwin
A Nightingale Sang in Berkeley Square
  Sherwin/Maschwitz (sung by Vera Lynn)
Maybe it's Because I'm a Londoner
  Hubert Gregg
The Streets of London Ralph McTell
Carnaby Street The Jam
London Calling The Clash
As I did Walk by Hampstead Fair Jethro Tull
Electric Avenue Eddie Grant
Baker Street Gerry Rafferty
Camden Town Madness
Chelsea Girl Simple Minds
Holloway Jail The Kinks
Mayfair Nick Drake
Oxford Street Everything But the Girl
Tower of London ABC
King's Cross Pet Shop Boys
Pentonville Babyshambles

In 1922 the BBC broadcast the first radio programme from the roof of Marconi House in the Strand, and 14 years later the first television programme was transmitted from Alexandra Palace.

Petrol-powered cars and buses became common.[7] Criminals were quick to catch on: Ruby Sparks and the 'Bobbed Hair Bandit' were among the first to use cars in smash-and-grab raids. Croydon Aerodrome became London's first airport in March 1920, with flights to Paris, Amsterdam and later Berlin – though flying was strictly for the rich and famous.[8]

But the 1920s brought hardship for most Londoners. Unemployment grew steadily and in May 1926 a row over wages in the coal industry turned into a nine-day General Strike. In London, so many workers joined in the strike that the army was called in to maintain order, while many ordinary Londoners kept the Underground and buses running.

7. By the end of the 1930s, 300,000 Londoners owned a car.
8. In 1930 Amy Johnson took off from Croydon to become the first woman to fly solo from Britain to Australia, a distance of over 17,500 km.

The collapse of New York's Wall Street stock market in 1929 led to a worldwide depression and, like the rest of the country, London suffered severe unemployment in the 1930s.

Across Europe, extreme politics flourished: Communism had plunged Russia into a bloody civil war, and now right-wing governments came to power in Germany, Italy and Spain. But, though the leader of the British Union of Fascists, Oswald Mosley, was a popular speaker, his party never won a seat in Parliament. When his Blackshirts tried to intimidate the Jewish population of the East End in 1936, they were forced back by roadblocks at the Battle of Cable Street (E1).

Though the Aliens Act of 1919 made it harder for refugees to find work, Russians and East Europeans arrived in large numbers in the 1920s, while 60,000 Jewish refugees came to London from Germany in the late 1930s. Many great talents made the city their home, including Sigmund Freud, the father of psychoanalysis; Sir Alexander Korda, the first film director to be knighted; and Nobel-prize-winning author Elias Canetti.

Speakers' Corner

There have always been places in London where public speaking was allowed, but the most famous is Speakers' Corner in the north-east corner of Hyde Park (close to Marble Arch). It was created in 1872 following a riot over laws against buying and selling on a Sunday. Famous speakers include:

- **Marcus Garvey,** black activist

- **Vladimir Ilyich Lenin,** later the first leader of the Soviet Union

- **Karl Marx,** author of the *Communist Manifesto*

- **George Orwell,** author of *1984* and *Animal Farm*

- **Christabel Pankhurst,** campaigner for women's rights

- **William Morris,** leader of the Arts and Crafts movement

- **Ben Tillett,** British socialist leader

- **Donald Soper, Baron Soper,** social activist and pacifist, nicknamed 'Dr Soapbox', who spoke at Speakers' Corner over 70 years, from 1926 to 1998.

It wasn't all misery in the 1930s – many homes had their first cars, vacuum cleaners, cookers and fridges. Women wore mass-produced dresses that copied the styles worn by film stars. People had more free time: working-class Londoners went to the cinema two or three times a week, watched football in one of the new stadiums or went to the races. Local councils encouraged sport for all with public football pitches, outdoor swimming pools and golf courses.

Meanwhile, London County Council moved thousands of London's poorer inhabitants from inner-city slums to the new sprawl of council flats on the outer edges of the city. As more and more Londoners went in search of a more 'rural' lifestyle, the suburbs continued to grow.

Park Royal Tube station, 1931, in the 'Streamline Moderne' style

The Blitz

When Nazi Germany invaded Poland on 1 September 1939, Britain declared war, and a Second World War was under way. For the first year, Londoners waited nervously for an attack that never came. Around 700,000 were evacuated from the city, mostly children. A similar number of adults left, but returned to the capital by Christmas – most were simply homesick or couldn't get used to country life.

Around 5 p.m. on 7 September 1940, this period of 'phoney' war ended with a very loud bang. The German Air Force, or Luftwaffe, dropped hundreds of bombs on the East End, killing 430 people. For the next eight months, up to 160 German aircraft rained bombs on the capital, night after night, dropping a total of 18,000 tonnes of high explosive. London's docks were a prime target, so the East End and the City bore the brunt of the attack. The worst of the attacks ended in May 1941, when Hitler switched his bombers to the eastern front to support 'Operation Barbarossa', an invasion of the Soviet Union.

The city was tested again in
January 1944, when
Germany launched
its V-l flying bombs,
nicknamed 'doodlebugs'.

V-1

These jet-powered missiles could be shot
down in the air, unlike the superfast V-2
rockets that replaced them. It was lucky the
war ended when it did, or the V-2s might have
forced a complete evacuation of London.

During the raids, many thousands of
Londoners headed for the relative safety of the
Underground stations. Millions more huddled
in six-person Anderson shelters made from
sheets of corrugated iron half-buried in the
garden. Every night, they wished their
neighbours good night and prayed they
would see the morning. During the day, the
survivors went about their business as best
they could, though their lives were now
regulated by ration books, clothing coupons
and identity cards.

Why didn't everyone panic? Perhaps after
centuries of fires, plagues and other disasters,
Londoners were quietly confident that the city

would survive. Or maybe they didn't like the idea of anyone pushing them around – especially that unspeakable Adolf Hitler.[9]

The Royal Family refused to budge: when Buckingham Palace took a direct hit, the Queen said: 'Now we can look the East End in the face.' Meanwhile, in the Cabinet War Rooms deep below Whitehall, Prime Minister Winston Churchill orchestrated the British war effort, often working from 8.30 a.m. until 3.00 the following morning.[10] Churchill had his faults, but he was the right man for the job, and Britons took him to their hearts.

The Blitz may have been London's finest hour, but by the end of the war 80,000 Londoners were dead or badly injured, 100,000 were homeless and 1.5 million homes had been destroyed. But at least London still looked like London – unlike the German capital Berlin, which was completely flattened.

9. Photographer David Bailey, whose family home was destroyed by a bomb, later recalled how he took it personally, even at the age of 7: 'A V-2 rocket knocked out a cinema in Upton Park where I used to go. . . . I thought Hitler had killed Mickey Mouse and Bambi.'
10. He recorded his stirring wartime speeches here. The rumour that the lines were actually spoken by actor Norman Shelley impersonating Churchill probably isn't true.

Buried London

- **Deep shelters.** Eight giant air-raid shelters were dug during the Second World War. Each shelter had two parallel tunnels about 427 m long and 5 m across, with bunks for 8,000 people. The shelters were meant to become part of a new underground express railway after the war, but the plan was dropped. You can see the entrance of one of the shelters, now named the Eisenhower Centre, near Goodge Street station.

- **Cabinet War Rooms.** Another complex under King Charles St (SW1) was Churchill's HQ in the Second World War. Hundreds of underground offices (some now open to the public) were linked to the Ministry of Defence in Whitehall.

- **The Bank of England**'s underground vaults have more floor-space than the City's tallest building, Tower 42 (formerly the NatWest Tower). Some 400 tonnes of UK government gold are stored here. According to legend, in the 1830s the directors were summoned to a meeting in the vaults in the middle of the night by a sewerman who had found a way in.

- **Wine stores.** Berry Brothers & Rudd, London's oldest wine merchants, have storage space in their cellars for 240,000 bottles. Below Harrods is a warren of tunnels used to store wines and other goods.

- **Water supply.** Built between 1988 and 1993, London's Water Ring Main is an 80 km system of concrete pipelines that deliver some 1,100,000,000 litres of water every day.

- **Caverns.** There are tunnels and caves all over Blackheath, but no-one really knows how old they are. In 1780, one large cave became a popular tourist spot until 19-year old Lucy Talbot fainted in the stuffy air below and died soon after. Undeterred, the owners dug a ventilation shaft and set up a notorious drinking club known as Jack Cade's Cave (after the 15th-century rebel leader), which was eventually shut down in 1854. The Beddington Caves below Plough Lane were a handy store for smugglers, even if they didn't run to Brighton as one legend suggested.

- **Underground cells.** Several dungeons survive from the 18th and 19th centuries, such as the Wood Street Compter in Russia Row (EC2).

- **Royal escape route.** There are several rumoured escape tunnels from Buckingham Palace. One is said to connect to the Piccadilly Tube line, giving the royals a speedy escape route to Heathrow. Another tunnel may run along the Mall, connecting the palace to a top-secret underground complex known unofficially as Q-Whitehall. In turn, this may be linked to the Defence Crisis Management Centre, a nuclear-bomb-proof bunker built below the Ministry of Defence in the 1990s.

Postwar London

At the end of World War II, the British economy was in a mess. The cost of fighting the war had left the government badly in debt. A year after the war was over, there were still 2 million men and women in uniform, all paid for by the government. Though the late 1940s was a grim time of food shortages, severe winters and wage freezes, the new Labour government was determined to get everyone back to work. By 1948 the economy started to pick up, helped by loans from the United States (finally paid back only in 2006).

That year, London was again home to the Olympics. The games were a budget affair – no new stadiums were built and the 4,000 athletes who took part all brought their own food and slept in military barracks – but they gave London and the world a much-needed boost after the war years.[11]

11. *Star of the games was Dutch sprinter Fanny Blankers-Koen, nicknamed the 'flying housewife', who won four gold medals. Seventeen-year-old American Bob Mathias won the decathlon, apparently just a few months after taking up the sport. When asked how he intended to celebrate his victory, he replied, 'I'll start shaving, I guess.'*

The 1950s were a boom period for Britain. Millions of new jobs were created for nurses, teachers and social workers. When Prime Minister Harold Macmillan said, 'Most of our people have never had it so good' in 1957, it wasn't far from the truth. People had more money in their pockets and lived longer. The upbeat mood was marked by the Festival of Britain in 1951, 'a tonic for the nation' that promoted the best in British art, design and technology. This confidence could also be seen in the Soho district of the West End, home to jazz clubs, illegal drinking dens, brothels and artists' studios.

St Paul's Cathedral
survived wartime bombing.

London immortalised

London and its districts have given their names to everything from beer to buns:

- **London pride.** A wild flower of the saxifrage family, as well as the name of a beer brewed in Chiswick.

- **London plane.** A symbol of London, this tall tree can thrive even in a soot-laden city. The waxy leaves are washed clean by the rain and the bark is shed regularly in large patches. Many planes planted 200 years ago are still going stong.

- **London broil.** This North American dish is usually made by grilling steak and then cutting it into thin strips. No-one knows how it got its name – it certainly isn't English!

- **Camberwell beauty.** This pretty butterfly got its name after it was discovered in Coldharbour Lane in Camberwell, south London, in August 1748.

- **Vauxhall cars.** Only one make of car gets its name from London: Vauxhall Motors built its first car in 1903 and its A-Type was one of the most successful cars in Britain before the First World War. In 1925 the company was bought by the American firm General Motors, but the name lives on.

- **Tooting Crater.** A 28-km-wide crater on Mars is named after the south London district where the astronomer who discovered it, Pete Mouginis-Mark, was born.

- **Chelsea bun.** A currant bun first created in the 18th century at the Bun House in Chelsea, which was popular with the royal family.

- **Lambeth Walk.** This song from the 1937 musical *Me and My Girl* is named after a market street in south London. In the late 1930s it inspired a dance craze in New York.

- **Hackney carriage.** In medieval times, the East London village of Hackney was already known for its horses, and later gave its name to the famous horse-drawn carriages. These were often overworked or forced to do boring, repetitive tasks, giving us the words 'hackneyed' and 'hack'.

By the end of the war, London's population had shrunk for the first time in hundreds of years. In fact, lots of new factories were struggling because the owners couldn't find enough workers. Between 1945 and 1947, over 345,000 Europeans came to work in Britain, including many Poles and Italians.

The destruction caused by the Blitz was a chance to get rid of the slums of the 1930s, and around 300,000 new homes were built every year from 1953 to 1957. Thousands of immigrants from former colonies in India, Pakistan and the Caribbean were invited to Britain to help rebuild the country. By 1961, 177,000 Caribbeans had arrived in London, changing the city forever.

Life wasn't easy for the new arrivals. Though some had special skills, such as nursing, many were young men who – due to lack of education and the prejudice of other Londoners – were often forced to accept dirty, poorly paid jobs. The large Caribbean population in the Notting Hill district of west London was targeted by racist 'Teddy Boys', leading to three days of street fighting.

And London still had to cope with the age-old problems of dirt and disease. The 'Great Smog' of December 1952, a suffocating mix of fog, smoke and pollution, caused the deaths of thousands of Londoners, but it also led to the 1956 Clean Air Act. This banned smoky fuels from the inner city and encouraged people to heat their homes with electricity and gas rather than coal fires.

When Queen Elizabeth II was crowned in 1953, three million people lined the streets of London to catch a glimpse of the new monarch. Twenty million more watched the ceremony for the first time on television. Many hoped it would mark a new era, especially now the years of rations and making do were over. Yet the 1960s and 70s brought even greater challenges to London. Would the fortunes of the old city finally begin to founder?

seven deadly deeds

- **Ratcliff Highway murders,** 1811. A vicious killer butchered Timothy Marr and three members of his household, then 12 days later cut the throats of a landlord, his wife and a barmaid at the nearby King's Arms tavern. The murders had taken place inside a locked building. The police arrested a sailor, John Williams, who hanged himself. His body was carried past the scene of the murders in a cart and buried with a stake through the heart.

- **Pimlico mystery,** 1886. Adelaide Bartlett was accused of killing her husband Edward using chloroform. As there was no evidence that she had given him a large dose, Mrs Bartlett was acquitted, though most were convinced of her guilt. The famous surgeon Sir James Paget joked that she should explain how she did it, 'in the interest of science'.

- **Acid murder,** 1887. Police arriving at 16 Batty Street found a woman who had died by having nitric acid forced down her throat. They also discovered Israel Lipski, an umbrella-stick salesman, hiding under her bed, with burns to his own throat. Despite intervention from rabbis and MPs, Lipski was hanged within a month. The incident led to a wave of anti-Jewish feeling.

- **Camden Town murder,** 1907. The death of Emily Dimmock at her home in Paul's Road (now Agar Grove, NW1) remains unsolved. Though Robert Wood was charged with murder, no-one was ever convicted. It was one of the first cases to be tried in the newly opened Old Bailey.

- **Dr Crippen,** 1910. When American Cora Crippen vanished into thin air, her husband claimed she had moved back to America due to an illness. But suspicions grew, and Dr Crippen decided to sail for America with his lover Ethel Le Neve. By now the story was big news, and the ship's captain recognised them, even though Le Neve was disguised as a boy. As the ship approached New York, Chief Inspector Dew from Scotland Yard, alerted by wireless telegraph, came out to meet them.

- **10 Rillington Place,** 1943–1945. When new tenants moved into the basement flat, three bodies were found in a hidden cupboard. The former tenant, John Christie, confessed to six murders, including that of his wife. Christie was hanged at Pentonville Prison. Rillington Place was by now so notorious that the houses were torn down and the road was renamed.

- **Ruth Ellis,** 1955. A night-club hostess, Ellis shot and killed her boyfriend, David Blakely, when he threatened to end their relationship. In a state of shock, she turned to Blakely's friend and said: 'Will you call the police, Clive?' Despite many calls for mercy, she was executed at Holloway on 13 July 1955 – the last woman to be hanged in Britain.

In the Swinging Sixties, London became the centre of fashion.

CHAPTER five

LONDON IS DEAD, LONG LIVE LONDON!

London since the sixties

I n the 1950s, young Londoners sat in envy as they watched American teenagers on the big screen driving their own cars, wearing the latest clothes and listening to the crazy new sound of Rock 'n' Roll.

Everything changed in 1964, when the Beatles conquered America. Suddenly Britain, and especially London, was the place to be.

The drab, grey attitudes of the 1950s were blown away by a wave of colour and creativity. 'Swinging London' was the capital of cool, from the space-age fashions of

Carnaby Street to the Rolling Stones rocking out in front of 500,000 people in Hyde Park. Young, modern and groovy was in, old was out. East End boys dated West End girls and 'normal' Londoners like actor Michael Caine and photographer David Bailey joined the ranks of the rich and famous. Meanwhile the hippies, famed for their long hair and unwashed clothes, said 'no' to money and normality, and 'yes' to peace, love and mind-altering drugs.

But London had changed in other ways. The boom time of the previous 200 years had come to a grinding halt, and by the early 1970s the party was over. The days of the British Empire were also numbered,[1] and the London docks, once the hub of the Empire, fell into serious decline.[2] Britain was struggling to keep up with its economic rivals.

1. From 1945 to 1965, the number of people under British rule outside the UK fell from 700 million to 5 million, most of them in Hong Kong.
2. The old London docks could not accommodate large modern container ships, which now docked downstream at Tilbury and Felixstowe. Between 1960 and 1980, all of London's docks closed, turning large parts of the East End into a wasteland – especially the Isle of Dogs, the site of today's Canary Wharf development.

London on the Silver Screen

The image of Swinging London led to a spate of films shot in the capital, including *A Hard Day's Night*, *Alfie*, *Blow-Up* and *The Italian Job*, all shot between 1964 and 1969. London has provided a backdrop for countless other movies:

- **Acton Lane Power Station** in *Aliens* (1986)
- **Battersea Power Station** in *Full Metal Jacket* (1987) and *The Dark Knight* (2008)
- **St James's Park** in *101 Dalmatians* (1996)
- **Westminster Bridge** and **Piccadilly Circus** in *28 Days Later* (2002)
- **King's Cross** in *The Ladykillers* (1955)
- **Thamesmead Estate** in *A Clockwork Orange* (1971)
- **St Bartholomew the Great** in *Four Weddings and a Funeral* (1994) and *Shakespeare in Love* (1998)
- **Selfridges** in *Love Actually* (2003)
- **Westminster Abbey** in *The Da Vinci Code* (2006)
- **Leadenhall Market** in *Harry Potter and the Philosopher's Stone* (2001)
- **The London Eye** in *Thunderbirds* (2004)
- **The British Museum** in *The Mummy* (1999)
- **The Hackney Empire** in *Chaplin* (1992)

Gambling and gangsters

Gambling has been popular in London since Roman times. By the 18th century there were 40 or so illegal gaming houses, nicknamed 'hells' and 'slaughterhouses', where wealthy aristocrats and criminals rubbed shoulders. Such clubs funded London's crime gangs, especially during the 1950s and 1960s.

Two of the most notorious gangs were run by the Kray twins in the East End and the Richardson brothers in South London.

The Krays owned a nightclub in the West End and hobnobbed with MPs, actors and film stars. Inevitably, the rival gangs came to blows as they fought to gain control of the clubs. After a decade of terror, in 1968 the Krays were arrested and tried for the murder of their associate Jack 'the Hat' McVitie in the Blind Beggar pub in Whitechapel. They were imprisoned for life.

The Richardson gang were sent to jail a year later for torturing their rivals (methods included nailing their victims to the floor or pulling their teeth out with pliers).

Down in the dumps

The 1970s were a time of doom and gloom for Londoners, marked by mass unemployment and bomb attacks by the Irish Republican Army (IRA).[3] The capital was crippled by a wave of strikes, especially during the 'Winter of Discontent' in 1978–1979.[4] High streets went into decline due to the growth of huge shopping malls on the outskirts of the city.

Factories closed down, unable to compete with foreign firms who took advantage of cheaper labour. By the 1970s, even London's famous red buses were made abroad.

During the 1960s, Londoners fed up with pre-war slums and dodgy landlords demanded better public housing. What they got was high-rise tower blocks and new suburbs such as Thamesmead, where 60,000 houses were

3. The IRA hoped that direct attacks on London and other targets in the UK would eventually reunite the island of Ireland, which had been divided into two countries in 1921: Northern Ireland (still in the UK) and the Republic of Ireland (now independent).
4. Among those on strike were the city's bin men. Westminster City Council even used Leicester Square in the West End to dump piles of rubbish, a feast for local rats.

built on drained marshland. The tower blocks quickly lost their futuristic look as the concrete turned from shiny white to grimy grey. Some were badly built: in 1967 the corner of one block, Ronan Point, collapsed, killing five people and injuring 17 others.

London reacted to the dreariness of the 70s in typically rebellious fashion: crowds of punks hung out along the King's Road in Chelsea, horrifying grannies with their safety pins, wild hairstyles and swearing. The Sex Pistols' 'God Save the Queen' did its best to offend royalists during the Queen's Silver Jubilee in 1977. Londoners had a new attitude towards authority, old-fashioned values and property.

Demonstrations were a regular sight. Workers, students, women and gays demanded their rights, while the Campaign for Nuclear Disarmament wanted to 'ban the bomb'. Many feared an all-out nuclear war between the Soviet Union and the United States.

Modern times

The election of Mrs Thatcher as Britain's first female prime minister in 1979 led to a change of government, but many problems from the 1970s spilled over into the new decade, including the IRA bombing campaign.[5] Race relations reached an all-time low in 1981 when tensions between the police and young black men led to the Brixton riots in south London. Up to 5,000 people joined in, black and white, torching more than 100 vehicles and damaging 150 buildings.

By now London had come a long way from the mainly white city of the 1960s. The 70s and 80s saw the arrival of Kenyan Asians, Vietnamese refugees, Greek and Turkish Cypriots, Chinese from Hong Kong, West Africans and Bangladeshis. Asian curry houses and corner shops and Chinese takeaways were soon a familiar – and popular – feature of London's streets.[6]

5. The campaign rumbled on into the early 1990s, when two huge bombs were detonated in the City and in Docklands, killing several people and causing millions of pounds of damage.
6. Today almost 50 per cent of Londoners eat a curry at least once a week.

In the early 1980s unemployment continued to rise, partly due to Mrs Thatcher's determination to shut down Britain's outdated manufacturing industry. The 'Iron Lady' also set out to crush left-wing organisations such as the trade unions. She fought and won against striking coal miners in 1984, and two years later abolished the Greater London Council (GLC). London was now the only large city in the world without a local government.

The boom times returned briefly in the mid-1980s. After the 'Big Bang' in 1986, finance went hi-tech and money poured in as banking replaced manufacturing. Gleaming office blocks sprang up in Docklands and in the 'Square Mile' of the old City of London. Many of the new buildings would have made Sir Christopher Wren turn in his grave. Property developers cashed in while those at the bottom of the ladder got left behind. Houses skyrocketed in value[7] – then crashed at the end of the decade, leaving many people badly in debt.

7. In February 1987, a 4 m x 2 m cupboard in a posh apartment block was sold for £36,500. For that price you could have bought a rather nice house in some parts of Britain.

In 1990, Mrs Thatcher introduced the Community Charge – widely known as the 'poll tax' – which hit rich and poor alike. Around 200,000 people from all over Britain marched on Trafalgar Square to protest. When mounted police officers and police vans charged at the crowd, tempers flared and a riot broke out. Shop windows were smashed, cars were overturned, and scuffles were still going on between demonstrators and police at 3 a.m. The rebellious side of London was alive and very much kicking, and by the end of the year Mrs Thatcher was forced to resign.

London has always been a global centre, but during the 1980s and 90s its connections to the rest of the world grew even stronger. By 1987 the city had five airports, at Heathrow, Gatwick, Stansted, Luton and Docklands, while 1994 saw the opening of the high-speed Eurostar rail link to Paris and Brussels. Travellers arrived at Waterloo Station, named after a British victory over the French in 1815 – welcome to London! Meanwhile, commuters spent hours whizzing (or in rush hour, crawling) around London on the M25 motorway, completed in 1986.

By the mid-1990s, London was hip again. Its clubs and bars attracted a new generation of tourists, and the capital again became a byword for fashion and street style. Love them or hate them, modern landmarks such as the Gherkin[8] and the Millennium Dome (now the O2 arena) gave the city a new look.

After Tony Blair and New Labour swept into power in May 1997, London was at last given its first city-wide mayor (in 2000). When Blair put forward his own candidate, Londoners promptly elected Ken Livingstone, the rebellious former leader of the GLC. His Congestion Charge – a toll paid by motorists in central London – reduced traffic by up to 20 per cent, but Londoners still moan about public transport more than almost anything else. The plan for the 2012 Olympics promises a raft of new shiny trains and services, but inevitably the traffic jams will remain.

So after 2,000 years, where is London now?

8. *Officially known as 30 St Mary Axe, and formerly the Swiss Re building – but nobody calls it by either of those names.*

London today

Though Londoners got richer in the 90s and 'noughties', their city has relatively more crime and more people sleeping rough on the streets than anywhere else in Britain. Many people, especially those in poor areas, don't trust the police. They worry about violent teenage gangs and drug dealing on the streets.

Some argue that the real London has vanished forever: modern developers have destroyed more of the old city than the Blitz ever did, they say, and the factories and docks that made London great have been replaced by ugly office buildings and retail parks. Meanwhile, many of the old working-class communities in the inner city have been driven to the suburbs by soaring rents.

But London has never stood still. It's growing again, to the point where it's hard to know where the city stops and the rest of the country begins. People commute into the city from Oxford, Brighton and Norwich,[9] and

9. *Apparently every minute spent on the train to London cuts £1,000 off the average house price!*

thanks to the Internet, Londoners can live anywhere. I live in Dublin now, but most of my work is back in London, and for many years I flew there every other week.

When the train from the airport hits town, you can feel everything moving up a gear. Dublin's no rural backwater, but I'm still shocked by the pace of London life – and the sheer scale of it. Like Victorians travelling into town by tram, I revel in going 'up West'. There's a special buzz around Soho that's hard to find anywhere else. It's partly the crowds, partly the awkward, narrow streets that come from a thousand years of bad planning.

My old London friends reflect the city's cosmopolitan nature, and its history: Rhiannon, born in west London but with Welsh and Polish blood flowing in her veins; Tooting Tone, born and bred south of the river; Marc and Thierry, who came from Yorkshire and France, both drawn by the lure of the big city; Sharon, whose parents came from Kenya and the West Indies in the 1970s as students and fell in love; and Martin, son of Irish migrants who arrived in the 1950s.

Sure, London has its problems. But as long as young people come in their droves to seek their fame and fortune, its success is guaranteed. I'm biased of course, but, in the words of songwriter Hubert Gregg:

Here's to the next 2,000 years!

Urban myths

Almost 900 years after Geoffrey of Monmouth told of Brutus battling local giants, Londoners still love a good story:

- A Victorian myth tells of ferocious 'black swine' living in the sewers of Hampstead (NW3) and feeding on the garbage washed into it. In recent times, the story has been changed: there is supposedly a race of flesh-eating humanoids living below London in a fabulous network of tunnels unknown to us ground-dwellers. Like vampires, they avoid the daylight and feed on a diet of vagrants and lost commuters!

- A story doing the rounds in the 1980s told of a group of men known as the 'Chelsea smilers'. Supposedly they went from school to school asking questions about Chelsea Football Club. Anyone who got the answer wrong would have their mouths cut open, creating scars in the shape of a permanent smile.

- The flush toilet was not invented by the 19th-century Londoner Thomas Crapper (though he did improve it by developing the ballcock), nor did his name give rise to a four-letter word, which was originally Dutch and probably arrived in England in Shakespeare's time, several hundred years earlier.

- The 'Maniac on the Platform' is an enduring urban myth about a serial killer who haunts crowded platforms on the Tube. No-one has ever seen him, but a friend of a friend told me that the mystery figure waits for a train to approach and then pushes his target onto the rails – to certain death!

- In another legend, a psychopath haunts nightclubs around London. After subtly injecting clubbers with a syringe, he leaves a note in their pocket. When they read it the next morning, it tells them they have been injected with a deadly disease. Spooky stuff!

- In the late 1830s, Londoners reported being attacked by a demon who could leap over walls and hedges thanks to springs in his boots. Other accounts describe a giant with sharp claws, blazing red eyes and the power to spit out blue flames. No-one was ever arrested or convicted, but by the end of 1838 the panic over 'Spring-Heeled Jack' had died down.

- In 2009 a woman reported seeing a black panther in south-east London. Large cats have supposedly been seen in other parts of England, such as the famous-but-elusive 'Beast of Exmoor' – but sceptics might be alerted by the fact that this sighting was in Catford...

London nosh

Jellied eels are a classic in the East End where they are still sold from street stalls, but they're easy enough to make yourself if you can get hold of fresh eels.

Serves 4

Ingredients:
- 900 g (2 lb) eels, skinned and boned
- 600 ml (1 pint) fish stock
- 1 onion
- 1 carrot
- 1 small stick celery, finely chopped
- 15 g (½ oz) gelatine
- ½ lemon
- 1 bouquet garni
- fresh herbs, chopped
- grated nutmeg

Method:
Place the eels skin side down on the table and sprinkle with a pinch of grated nutmeg, grated lemon zest and the chopped herbs.

Cut each eel into pieces about 10 cm (4 in) long. Roll up each piece and tie with string. Put the stock, vegetables and bouquet garni into a saucepan and bring to the boil. Add the eels and simmer very gently for about 30 minutes or until tender.

Remove the eels, taking off the string, and place them in a bowl. Measure the stock and make up to 450 ml (¾ pint) with water. Add the lemon juice to the gelatine to dissolve, then add this to the hot stock. Stir until completely dissolved. Strain over the eels and leave to set.

Turn out when cold, and bingo! a ready-made Cockney feast. Serve with green salad and sliced gherkins.

- **Pie & mash** first became popular in the 18th century. In those days, pies were filled with eels caught in the Thames. Today, they are more likely to be filled with lamb or beef. The pie is served with lashings of mashed potato covered with a big spoonful of 'liquor', made from parsley and the juice left over from boiling eels.

- **Whitebait.** Perhaps the closest thing to a traditional south London dish were the whitebait dinners popular in Greenwich in Victorian times.

- **Bubble & squeak**, a traditional fry-up of leftover cabbage and potato, was especially popular after the Second World War, but is rarely found on menus today.

- **Pease pudding** was another East End favourite, a mushy dish of dried split peas soaked and boiled with butter then pushed through a sieve. It was usually served with ham or pork. If that sounds appetising, you might want to forget that in Cockney rhyming slang, 'pease pudding hot' meant 'snot'!

Seven London icons

- **FX4 taxi.** All drivers must pass a special test before they can drive one of the capital's famous black cabs. To pass 'the Knowledge' can take 2 to 4 years and involves learning 320 routes (or 'runs') within a 10 km radius of Charing Cross.

- **Routemaster.** the much-loved 'step-on, step-off' bus was introduced in 1956 and made its last journey in London on 9 December 2005.

- **Beefeaters.** Officially the Yeomen Warders of Her Majesty's Royal Palace and Fortress the Tower of London. Famous for their red and gold Tudor-style uniforms, they've been guarding the Tower since 1485.

- **Tube map.** Harry Beck created a simplified map in 1931 after realising that travellers were interested in getting from one station to another rather than knowing exactly where the stations were on the surface.

- **Red telephone boxes.** Sir Giles Gilbert Scott's classic design, the K3, first appeared in 1929. Once a familiar sight on London's streets, they are now few and far between. In the 1980s thousands of boxes were sold off – some were even converted into shower cubicles!

- **Pearly Kings and Queens.** Roadsweeper Henry Croft came up with the idea of covering a suit with rows of shiny buttons in the early 1880s, in order to collect money for charity. Today's Pearly Kings and Queens continue this tradition, wearing outfits inspired by the dress of Victorian costermongers (see page 116).

- **Bearskins.** The Changing of the Guard that takes place on the forecourt of Buckingham Palace at around 11 a.m. is the best time to catch the red uniform and tall fur cap of the Queen's Foot Guards. The standard bearskin is 46 cm tall, weighs 700 g, and is made from the fur of the Canadian black bear.

Ten things you didn't know about London's landmarks

1. **British Museum.** The painted coffin lid of an ancient Egyptian priestess was given to the museum after the tourists who bought it all had nasty accidents on the way home. The delivery man died within a week and a photographer was so spooked that he killed himself. Later (false) rumours suggested that the 'unlucky' artefact had been sold to an American and was on the *Titanic* when it went down. Look for exhibit no. 22542 and decide for yourself whether it is cursed.

2. **Tower Bridge.** In December 1952 the bridge opened while a No. 78 bus was on it. Driver Albert Gunter put his foot down and jumped across a metre-wide gap. Luckily, there were no serious injuries.

3. **Waterloo Station.** In 1854, during a major outbreak of cholera, the London Necropolis Company operated a daily 'funeral service' to Brookwood cemetery in Surrey. It had a bar with a sign saying 'Spirits served here'!

4. **BT Tower.** Despite being 189 m tall and a familiar London landmark, for almost 30 years the tower was officially a secret (and did not appear on maps) until MP Kate Hoey confirmed its address – 60 Cleveland St – in Parliament on 19 February 1993.

5. **Canary Wharf Tower,** the tallest building in London, is named after a quay owned by a

firm that traded with the Canary Islands. By coincidence, the Canaries are named after the dogs (in Latin: *canes*) that lived there, while the Docklands area is known as the Isle of Dogs, perhaps because it was the site of King Henry VIII's hunting kennels.

6. **London Eye.** On a clear day, you can see places up to 40 km away, including Windsor Castle. The Eye rotates at 0.9 km/h – twice as fast as a sprinting tortoise, it's said!

7. **Westminster Abbey.** About 3,300 people are buried here, including Charles Darwin, Sir Isaac Newton and Dr David Livingstone. There's a memorial to Sir Winston Churchill.

8. **Covent Garden.** Designed in 1632 by Inigo Jones, the famous piazza has always been a place of entertainment. In 1662 Samuel Pepys watched the first recorded Punch and Judy show in England here, performed by the Italian showman 'Signor Bologna'.

9. **Big Ben.** The 98 m clock tower next to the Houses of Parliament isn't actually called Big Ben, but its giant hour bell is. It may be named after Benjamin Caunt, a champion boxer who was known for being big but slow!

10. **Marble Arch.** The arch was originally built as the entrance to Buckingham Palace but not used. Inside is a tiny office which used to be a police station. On the traffic island nearby is a plaque marking the site of Tyburn Tree, where about 50,000 criminals were hanged.

Ten alternative days out

1. Walk around the gardens of Down House in Bromley, where Charles Darwin wrote his revolutionary book on evolution, *On the Origin of Species* (1859).

2. Take a tour of Wembley Stadium, England's national football ground, and discover the history of this sporting mecca.

3. Catch a show at Hackney Empire, where Charlie Chaplin, Stan Laurel and W. C. Fields all trod the boards a century ago.

4. Visit the Fan Museum in Greenwich, the only one of its kind in the world.

5. See, hear and even play musical instruments from around the world at the Horniman Museum in Forest Hill.

6. Go bird-spotting at Europe's largest wetland creation project, the WWT London Wetland Centre in Barnes.

7. Take the plunge in England's largest open-air pool at Tooting Bec Lido, built in 1906.

8. Get back to nature at Mudchute Farm on the Isle of Dogs, the UK's largest urban farm.

9. Visit Singh Sabha Gurdwara in Southall, the largest Sikh temple outside India.

10. Check out the Thames Barrier at Woolwich Reach and decide for yourself if it can protect London from rising sea levels.

Wild about the city?

- Over 40 per cent of London is green space or open water. The city is home to 2,000 species of flowering plant, 47 species of butterfly, 1,173 moths and more than 270 kinds of spider, as well as squirrels, foxes and deer. Some 120 species of fish live in the Thames.

- Rats and eels live in the old sewer tunnels. Though they say you are never more than a few metres away from a rat, it is rare to see one.

- Until recently, mosquitoes only lived in warm Underground tunnels, but milder winters and the growth of patio heaters have brought them into the open.

- The famous pigeons of Trafalgar Square are descendants of wood pigeons that arrived during the 19th century. In 2000, Mayor Ken Livingstone declared war on the pigeons. Loud-hailers and klaxons were used to terrify the birds and huge vacuum machines sucked up the seeds left out for them. Hawks were used to scare off or kill the pigeons.

- There are some 200 species of bird in Greater London, including escaped parrots. Seagulls only arrived in 1891, attracted by the warmth of the city during a particularly cold winter.

- There are about 700,000 dogs in London. In 1900 there were 750,000 cats and over 250,000 working horses, producing over a million tonnes of dung a year.

Rhyming slang and Estuary English

Rhyming slang was probably invented by London's street traders, or costermongers, in the 1840s. They replaced a common word with a phrase that rhymed with it, allowing them to speak to each other without their customers (or the police) being able to understand them.

Here are some classic phrases:

- **apples and pears** — stairs
- **Barnet Fair** — hair
- **bubble bath** — laugh*
- **butcher's hook** — look
- **dog and bone** — telephone
- **trouble and strife** — wife
- **whistle and flute** — suit

Some use the names of famous people:

- **Sexton Blake** (fictional detective) — fake
- **Ruby Murray** (singer) — curry
- **Britney Spears** (singer) — beers
- **Tod Sloan** (jockey) — own
- **Harry Randall** (music-hall comedian) — candle

Often only the first part of the phrase is used, as in 'Let's have a butcher's' or 'She's all on her tod.'

*Yes, this does rhyme in East End pronunciation.

In recent years, 'Estuary English' has been London's revenge on the rest of the country as celebrities fall over themselves to speak in a fake Cockney or 'Mockney' accent. To follow the trend, simply pronounce 'mother' as if it's got two 'v's. But if you want to sound like a real Londoner, block your ears to the following:

- **Dick Van Dyke**'s 'Gawd bless you' twang in the movie *Mary Poppins* (1964) is about as natural-sounding as a Dalek screaming 'Exterminate, exterminate.'

- **Johnny Depp** is said to have modelled his accent in *Pirates of the Caribbean* (2003) on Keith Richard, guitarist of the Rolling Stones and a native of Dartford. But it's a case of Dorset meets Dagenham as his accent wanders around Britain from one line to the next.

- **Don Cheadle** is a fine actor and apparently worked long and hard to perfect his London accent in *Ocean's 11* (2001). Not long and hard enough, unfortunately.

- **Audrey Hepburn** is great fun to watch in *My Fair Lady* (1964), but never nails the accent. Luckily Stanley Holloway, who once worked as a clerk in Billingsgate fish market, is on hand to show how it's done in his role as Alfred P. Doolittle.

Glossary

alderman A member of a city council.

amphitheatre An oval Roman stadium with tiered seats.

basilica In Roman times, a large hall used for public meetings.

Blitz The sustained German bombing of British cities, especially London, between 7 September 1940 and 10 May 1941, during the Second World War.

Celts A group of peoples who spread across Europe from around 400 BC.

cesspit An underground pit for storing sewage, in a place where there are no modern drains.

City of London The part of London once surrounded by the medieval city walls. Known as 'the City', it is now London's banking and finance centre.

Cockney A term usually used to describe working-class Londoners from the East End, but in theory any Londoner born within the sound of the bells of the Church of St Mary-le-Bow.

coronation The ceremony of crowning a new king or queen.

cosmopolitan Made up of people or things from all over the world.

forum In Roman times, an open space used as a marketplace and for holding public meetings.

gallows A wooden frame used for hanging criminals.

guild A group of craftworkers in a particular trade.

heath An area of land left in its natural state, not used for building or farming.

immigrant A person who comes to work or live in a country where they were not born.

Industrial Revolution The rapid development of industry that began in the late 18th century.

Irish Republican Army (IRA) A group of Irish nationalists who tried to drive British forces out of Northern Ireland using terrorism and guerilla warfare.

mark A weight of silver, usually worth £⅔ (13s. 4d.).

metropolis Any large city.

Metropolitan Police The London police force, founded in 1829.

Neanderthals The extinct cousins of modern humans, who disappeared around 30,000 BC.

Parliament The British government, or the building where it meets.

pea-souper A nickname for thick London fog or smog (a mixture of smoke and fog), so called because of its thick texture and greenish colouring.

plague A deadly disease spread by infected fleas that live on rats.

playhouse An old name for a theatre.

poll tax A tax that is the same for everyone, rich or poor.

refugee Someone who has to leave their home for their own safety, often going to another country.

Romano-Britons Ancient Britons who had adopted Roman customs.

sack To destroy completely (an enemy city).

siege The act of surrounding an enemy city in order to force it to surrender.

skyline The outline of a city's tall buildings.

slums Poor, overcrowded and often dirty housing.

suburb A district on the outskirts of a city.

Suffragette A woman who campaigned for the right of women to vote.

Timeline of London history

c.450,000 BC Thames diverted into its present valley.

c.400,000 BC First humans live in Thames Valley.

c.60,000 BC Neanderthals hunt mammoths and other prehistoric animals in Thames Valley.

c.40,000 BC Modern humans first appear.

c.13,000 BC Modern humans settle permanently in the Thames Valley.

c.3900–3500 BC First buildings in Thames Valley. Also many earth and timber monuments built in areas cleared of woodland.

c.2000 BC Arrival of farming in Thames Valley.

c.500 BC Celtic culture spreads across England.

55–54 BC Julius Caesar invades Britain twice, but after brief campaigns returns to Gaul (France).

AD 43 Roman invasion of Britain begins.

50 Romans found London, naming it Londinium, and build first bridge across the Thames.

60 Boudicca revolts, burning London to the ground.

61–122 Londinium rebuilt; becomes a thriving city.

120 Great fire in London (the first of many).

c.180 First stone walls built around city.

c.250 London flourishing, with population of 45,000.

407 Roman army leaves Londinium.

c.460 Romano-Britons flee from city due to threat from Anglo-Saxon invaders.

490 Saxons take charge of London.

c.600 Saxons build a new town, Ludenwic, in the area near Covent Garden and the Strand.

604 St Paul's Cathedral first built.

c.650 Saxon Ludenwic now a prosperous town and port with some 10,000 inhabitants.

842 First attack by Vikings on London.

851 London looted by Viking raiders.

886 Saxon King Alfred recaptures the city after a three-year siege.

880s Ludenwic is abandoned and Saxons build new town within the old Roman walls.

941 Great fire destroys much of Saxon London.

1013–1016 London survives sieges by Danish kings Sweyn Forkbeard and Cnut, but is forced to pay tax.

1018 Tax payment shows London by far the wealthiest English town – and it's been no. 1 ever since.

1052 Edward the Confessor builds Westminster Palace and rebuilds Westminster Abbey (finished 1065).

1066 William the Conqueror is crowned at Westminster.

1078 William builds White Tower to guard London.

1123 Rahere founds St Bartholomew's, first hospital.

1127 First Guildhall built.

1176 First stone bridge across the Thames.

c.1191 London has its first Mayor, Henry Fitz Aylwin.

1290 Jews forced to leave London.

1348 Black Death kills one third of Londoners.

1381 Peasants' Revolt put down in London.

1397 Dick Whittington becomes Mayor.

1535–1539 Henry VIII loots and destroys many of London's monasteries and churches.

1571 The Royal Exchange is built.

1580 150,000 people now living in London.

1599 Globe Theatre is built in Southwark.

1637 Hyde Park is opened to the public by Charles I.

1649 Charles I executed at Whitehall.

1652 First coffee house opens in London.

1660 London home to 500,000 people.

1665 Great Plague sweeps through London.

1666 Great Fire destroys most of medieval city.

1670 West End becomes a fashionable place to live.

1694 Bank of England founded.

1712 St Paul's Cathedral rebuilt after Great Fire.

1750 Westminster Bridge built. Bow Street Runners formed, an early police force.

1780 Gordon Riots last for six days.

1801 London's population reaches 1 million.

1809 Gas lamps light Pall Mall.

1816 Spitalfields Riots.

1819 Piccadilly Circus built, hub of new West End.

1829 Sir Robert Peel founds Metropolitan Police Force.

1831 Cholera outbreak devastates London.

1834 Fire destroys Houses of Parliament.

1837 Queen Victoria moves into Buckingham Palace. Euston opens, first intercity railway station.

1851 Crystal Palace houses Great Exhibition.

1858 'Great Stink' leads to creation of a modern sewer system in London.

1859 Clock tower housing Big Ben is completed.

1860s Large music halls increasingly popular.

1863 Metropolitan line opens, world's first underground railway.

1871 3 million people in London. Albert Hall is built.

1878 Electric lighting first appears in city.

1888 Jack the Ripper begins his reign of terror.

1899 London County Council formed.

1892 Blackwall Tunnel built under the Thames.

Timeline of London History

1894 Tower Bridge is built.

1901 Over 6 million people living in London.

1903 First council houses built in city.

1906 Suffragettes hold protest in Parliament Square. Harrods' landmark store built in Knightsbridge.

1908 Olympic Games held in London.

1915 German Zeppelins drop first bombs on London.

1922 BBC broadcasts the first radio programme from Marconi House on the Strand.

1923 Wembley Stadium is built.

1926 General Strike.

1936 Battle of Cable St between Fascists and opponents.

1940–1941 German bombers devastate East End during the Blitz.

1948 London holds Olympics for second time. MS *Empire Windrush* lands first large group of West Indian immigrants at London's Tilbury docks.

1951 Festival of Britain held on South Bank.

1952 Great Smog kills thousands of Londoners.

1955 Heathrow Airport opens.

1958 Notting Hill race riots.

1965 Creation of Greater London Council (GLC). Post Office (now BT) Tower completed.

1969 Rolling Stones perform in Hyde Park.

1973 IRA begins bombing campaign.

1981 Brixton rxiots.

1985 M25 motorway around London is finished.

1987 Canary Wharf in Docklands is built.

1990 Poll Tax riots

1994 Channel Tunnel links London to Europe.

2000 London Eye built. City elects first citywide Mayor.

2012 London holds Olympics for third time.

Index

NB: 'n' after a page number indicates a footnote

Other titles in
The Cherished Library

Ancient Egypt
A Very Peculiar History
The Art of Embalming:
Mummy Myth and Magic
With added Squishy Bits
Jim Pipe
ISBN: 978-1-906714-92-5

Brighton
A Very Peculiar History
With added Hove, actually
David Arscott
ISBN: 978-1-906714-89-5

Ireland
A Very Peculiar History
With NO added Blarney
Jim Pipe
ISBN: 978-1-905638-98-7

Rations
A Very Peculiar History
With NO added Butter
David Arscott
ISBN: 978-1-907184-25-3

Heroes, Gods and Monsters of
Ancient Greek Mythology
Michael Ford
ISBN: 978-1-906370-92-3

Scotland
A Very Peculiar History
With NO added Haggis
or Bagpipes
**Vol. 1: From ancient times
to Robert the Bruce**
ISBN: 978-1-906370-91-6

**Vol. 2: From the Stewarts
to modern Scotland**
ISBN: 978-1-906714-79-6

Fiona Macdonald

The Blitz
A Very Peculiar History
With NO added Doodlebugs
David Arscott
ISBN: 978-1-907184-18-5

Wales
A Very Peculiar History
With NO added Laverbread
Rupert Matthews
ISBN: 978-1-907184-19-2

Heroes, Gods and Monsters of
Celtic Mythology
Fiona Macdonald
ISBN: 978-1-905638-97-0

The Cherish Family

The Cherish Brothers

The Cherished Library is a definitive collection of masterworks, beautifully written and stunningly designed and illustrated by the most influential authors, artists, designers and bookbinders of their day.

These facsimile editions from the world-class collection of the Cherish Family Library have been lovingly crafted to recreate the authentic look and feel of the originals in the family's much-loved library.*